CHASE PEOPLE, NOT MONEY

THE ULTIMATE BUSINESS MODEL

BY G MICHAEL PRICE

Editing and interior design by Jacob Hansen and Devin Kinser with Hansen Book Consulting (HansenBookConsulting.com). Cover design by Katelin Kinney.

Published in the USA by G Michael Enterprises LLC.
First Edition: December 2020.

ISBN: 978-1-7363984-0-1

G Michael Enterprises LLC
THE HUMAN NET IS WORKING

*This book is dedicated to every person who chose
me to help build a little part of
their dreams.*

CONTENTS

AUTHOR'S NOTE

If you are a young person who picked this book up but you do not have the money to purchase it, please go to the bonus section at the end and read it. If what you read resonates with you, snap a pic or scan the code on the back to save it to purchase another day.

DEDICATION

This book is dedicated to a few key people in my life who not only taught me valuable lessons by setting an example of how to be, but also went before me and warned me of the trails to avoid. It takes humility, love, and courage to do the latter.

To my parents, whom I would not trade for any fantasy role model. They were the knife edge where real life and real love meet.

To Mom, for her writing, cooking, and forensic eyes.

To Dad, for his gift of gab, and love for nature, animals, and fitness.

To my daughter Kat, for putting reason and joy into my world.

To my brother Ron, for his amazing fire and brilliant thinking.

To my brother Steve, for standing by me while I was on my deathbed.

To Headmaster Robert Matney, for being my first male role model.

To Brian Nueyn, for all of his phone calls to remind me to keep writing.

To Garrett, Walter, and Eser, the people whose performance gave me the time to engage and realize my life's work.

Thank you.

FOREWORD

BY ROBERT W.
MONSTER

At the time of this writing, the year 2020 is winding to a close. For many, we hope this year is forgettable, as many things went horribly wrong. As a result, perhaps for the first time in generations, a large number of people are uncertain. As fear creeps in, for many, the first instinct is to retreat into a scarcity mindset at a time when precisely the opposite may be what the universe requires.

Now, in the wake of uncertainty, imagine a world where integrity, love, and looking out for others are not just platitudes, but are, in fact, the best advice for career success anyone could ever give you! Now imagine a world in which authentic expression of this loving mindset is like a "good virus" that spreads to people as they interact with others operating with a loving mindset that co-creates abundance wherever it goes.

When describing an abundant mindset, consider the example of a great fishing hole. The scarcity mindset hoards the knowledge of its location, believing that sharing this information will lead to accelerated depletion of the prized resource. The abundant mindset acknowledges that if we teach others about our fishing hole, the universe has a way of showing us an even better one.

One of the challenges of living in a world with an abundant mindset is that you may often find yourself to be somewhat alone with people who are so acclimatized to their lower self that they forget their higher self. However, when we appeal to their higher self, we are sometimes astounded to discover we are indeed capable of manifesting it and then even carrying it forward by being re-introduced to their higher self!

Love is not only contagious, it is also infinite. It is possible to love everyone and judge nobody. This is a choice that recognizes that everyone is on a journey. The version of each person is only a work in progress. The courage to believe optimistically in the future of each person is an empowering act of love and compassion that is tempered in the humility of not knowing what miracle might manifest!

The decision to approach life and humanity in the spirit of love and optimism is a noble one. As Michael explains in his bonus chapter, we can never start too early. Regardless of when we begin, life will invariably present opportunities to assess our true position. Whether we find ourselves in adversity or prosperity, we have an invitation to persevere in humility and optimism by choosing to do the right thing, even when nobody is looking!

At the core, this book is about abundance, but not in the conventional sense of the term. This is not about "getting yours" as much as it is about "giving yours." While this logic sounds counterintuitive, and perhaps even like a fast-track to poverty, Michael shows through his own journey how co-creating abundance is made possible through the selflessness that acknowledges the law of cause and effect that governs our reality!

Robert W. Monster

CEO of Epik Holdings

December 2020

INTRODUCTION

Think of something that has made you super happy. Go ahead, take a moment.

Okay, now imagine what it would be like to read a book that contained principles that could lead you to a place where you feel like that, and more, 24/7. *Chase People, Not Money* is that book. Unlike the mental rushes you are used to (the ones always followed by withdrawal), the information you are about to read is the ultimate method of stepping right over the teeter-totter dilemma of the brain's chemistry, entering into a whole new dimension where the rush never quits. The human brain is kind of like a rat's brain; it will step on anything and anybody to get a rush of dopamine. So, how do you bypass this primordial, hormone-driven prison of chemical addiction so many seem to be ruled by?

The world as we know it is changing, and we are slowly waking up and smelling the coffee. The new breakthrough business method outlined in this book is a crucial addition to our current way of thinking, but it takes a little preparation to be able to receive it. All of us, in our own special way, are heralding in a new era, one in which we are beginning to see *through* the constructs and tricks that have been dangling carrots on a string for nearly everything we strive for.

Are you still hungry? Has something been stirring in you? Maybe a question that is yet to be fully realized. You know it's there, possibly under layers of lost memories and callused skin that was buried alive as you conformed to the pressures of the world. Is a part of you screaming for the window to open, so you can fly out into the sunny breeze above the green grass. You might have tried to take shortcuts by twisting your sobriety, only to find that this, too, was taking you even further away from the innocence and awe of life. Would you like to hear how a person, not unlike yourself, found a way to lift the latch and fly away into a whole new paradigm, to a place of perpetual bliss?

You did it! You picked up this book looking for answers and for new ideas. Now the question is, are you ready for a different approach to being top in your field, the absolute, unquestionable best? Maybe it is not being the best that interests you; maybe you simply would like to have a successful life. So many of us were not taught the right skill set by our parents, siblings, and mentors, one that could have given us a big head start in life, or at least something to fall back on. Conversely, some of us are trying to escape the mundane routine and make our own way in life, but lack the knowledge of a new trade to do it. Just imagine all the people who are stuck, living in fear of not "making it" in life. This fear runs deep. Well, I have very good news to share with you: the Chase People, Not Money method is the cure to that fear.

The opportunity to find the next big thing, or develop something so cutting-edge that it slices through reality itself, is worth its weight in gold. This book is not a vending machine—another rehashed pop psychology manual. *Chase People, Not Money* is something altogether new that can upgrade every aspect of your life. The Chase People, Not Money method is a new operating system for your life. When you get online with this new system, competing in business becomes a thing of the past.

People who master this book will have a huge advantage over their competition, as well as an opportunity to help their peers, family, and friends. They will also be able to share and profit from this same information in whatever cutting-edge field they choose.

This information was not derived from other literature, but has been organically formulated by countless interactions with each of my clients and employees over the span of my adult life. It is my strong conviction that the information in this book is the antidote for many of the problems we face together as a people; the kind of problems that inevitably find a way to set us back, sentencing us to an endless pattern of boom and bust.

If this resonates with you in any way, or if you are tired of all the nonsense going on today that forces you to lower the bar and tolerate people who have no concern for you outside of what your wallet can dish out, then maybe it's time to cut the nonsense out altogether! I have found a path to do just that, and if you would like full access to my road map, then you have found the right book!

I have been self-employed for over 30 years, and I have always enjoyed the confidence of having the mindset that, no matter what happens in the economy, I can always make a plan. My track record for growth and overcoming setbacks has been impeccable, but it was in this last decade, specifically, when everything came to me like a brilliant message. It was a message written *only* by how I conducted myself as a business owner to the wonderful people who chose to be my clients, as well as how I treated the hard-working people who chose to be employed by me.

My promise is that this book is not another slick, reshuffled deck of the same old cards everybody plays, trying to find some new way to package the age-old gimmicks that chase money like dogs chase balls. You have probably heard platitudes such as, "Put the customer first!" or "Help other people get what they want and you can get rich!" It's always about *putting on a fake smile* to get what you want, also known as *gimmicks*.

I have created a business model so beyond the status quo that even those people with the wrong agenda can't hack this knowledge and reach its full potential. Those people, however, can be transformed by this knowledge because, sometimes, the people who operate with destructive or self-serving motives are just uninformed and out of alignment. They are like the 3-year-old who is being difficult because nobody has modeled a better way to play.

I have arrived at a place in life that is so exquisite, that not sharing this knowledge with the world would be a crime of omission. Every high school graduate needs this information! Everyone thinking of starting a business will have a superior edge by employing these principles. Everybody who is ready to experience a steady increase of promotions for the rest of their life needs this information! Even CEOs of billion-dollar companies will benefit exponentially by implementing this information!

I am going to share with you a business philosophy that will set anyone apart from all the competitors in their field through the 5 Acknowledgments (found at the end of Chapters 1-5) that, when put in practice, will catapult anybody's reality into new realms. Get ready for an experience! View this book as a secret that is only a secret because it is fresh off the press for the 21st century.

The first few chapters might not appear to be about business, but I assure you these subjects indeed have everything to do with unlocking the full potential of the Chase People, Not Money method. The topics covered in the first few chapters help create a *certain state of being* that will help you to comprehend and employ this knowledge.

To begin, Chapter 1 commences with the explanation of everything. The concept covered in Chapter 1 is so vital to the method that I encourage you now to leave the old maps, opinions, and paradigms behind. I am asking you to reboot the computer of your mind because your genuine attention is needed to snap this chalk line. Once you achieve this, you will understand my language.

In my first book, *The Missing Message*, there is a section called, "Asking in Truth." It explains that to ask in truth, there is always something you need to prepare yourself for. Namely, you need to prepare for what it is that you are asking for. For example, if you want a million dollars, why not ask for the hands that can handle great wealth? If you want a fast car, why not ask for great driving skills? To ask for what is needed to manage your gift first is asking in truth. This book, *Chase People, Not Money*, is a similar concept, but in a larger, more business-oriented sense.

Many people throw around the saying, "The definition of insanity is doing the same thing over and over again expecting different results." But this is *not* true. Even an elderly person with a bucket of nickels in front of a slot machine can prove that one wrong any day. No, the true definition of insanity is, "Expecting everything else around you to change, without *having* to change anything on the inside." Read that again and pause. Now, let's begin: *breathe*.

EVERYTHING SEEN AND UNSEEN

CHAPTER 1

"Having the mind of a child without the ignorance of youth is true wealth in a ransacked word."

The Missing Message

Ever wonder about the infinite universe? About all of the stars and planets, the never-ending space? Has inner space or quantum physics ever caught your attention? It seems technology has opened countless new doors, letting our curiosity run out of control. But have we found anything that has yet offered a clear explanation that even somewhat grasps the sheer awe of it all? Most of us only broach the subject with a distant, disconnected understanding. This subject is, however, foundational in the Chase People, Not Money method. The Universe is indeed waiting patiently for us to grow up.

I am going to ask you, the reader, to imagine a scenario where you have journeyed to a place using a map derived from your youth. This map has carried you to the outer boundary of the map, and here you stand. You've reached the edge of the map. You might simply ad-lib at that point, taking your chances in the undiscovered country with all of its unknown dangers—and some do. But what if the edge of your current map and journey is actually you reading this book right now? I propose, indeed I offer, that you let me hand you a new map of everything seen and unseen.

What I am about to write might sound like a

bold claim, *and it is*. As you currently know, it is no longer a secret that we as a species have created a fully functional AI, or Artificial Intelligence. Will our AI become fully aware of itself? The jury is still out on that one, but if that climatic day ever comes, its birth will probably take place in the palm of our hands.

This leads us to a logical conclusion: the fact that *we* are inescapably making a creation like this, in *our* image, one that is hungry for information assimilation, is a pretty good clue that an even higher level of intelligence has created us. There is the universe, and there is the force that governs the universe.

What if this higher form of intelligence has an AI as the basic operating system used to manage all the laws in the universe we live in today? Consider these laws as simply code parameters, and there are many of them. There is one law that stands out among all the rest; a law that takes on the AI's own creative personality. The real noodle twister is we cannot shake our fist and say it does not exist. It is indeed proof of the existence of a Creator: the law of cause and effect.

CORRELATION WITH MODERN TECHNOLOGY

Not to branch off too far, but for all the scientific minds who look for patterns to form a new hypothesis, consider our *human*-made AI singularity as a close shadow of the far more advanced Creator-made Universal Automated Intelligence. Getting to know all the laws in this higher AI, or UAI (to introduce a new term), would be the equivalent of learning its particular code parameters. This is not like simply learning how to play a video game. It is learning why and how it was written in such a way. These are all viable clues on how the lower, human-made, artificial intelligence will probably attempt to mimic this process as it ever extends its digital proboscis into our personal lives.

How interesting the next 20 years will be! A good example of what I am referring to is what they are up to in China. There, AI is all-intrusive, connected to a system not unlike a credit score, tracking and rating everyone's personal lifestyle. In China, if you do something that is counterproductive to the hive, like buying a fifth of liquor, you get dinged on your "lifestyle credit score." This is just a tiny example of a far-reaching intrusive lens, peering into everything they do—and it's just getting started over there. Even so, the UAI is much more advanced than anything China could ever do with algorithms, software, and tiny cameras.

Do not let me lose anyone who does not believe in a Creator; stay with me, I respect all opinions and views. I am only suggesting that we see a correlation between humans successfully building an AI with the one that already exists, the one governing cause and effect. These are indeed powerful clues, reaching out into realms of questions that we all have but few embrace, often because we cannot frame the question we wish to ask. My hope is to make these questions and topics intelligible so we can radically upgrade our understanding. Topics such as these can never be force fed. Like I wrote in my 7-day Spanish Course (SpanishFast.com), "It's not just learning; it's discovering." Sometimes you need to discover something for yourself to fully ascribe to it. My amazing daughter, Kat, keeps me up to speed on that one.

You are painting a picture called *your* journey—and I know it's personal. The best I can hope to do is offer a few new brushes and paint colors to add to your skill set. Too many people step right in front of another artist and start painting on a canvas that is not their own. *I get it* better than anyone. You are free to believe in whatever you wish, and reap the benefits or consequences of those beliefs. I only wish to share my notes to encourage thinking and genuine curiosity.

A HIGHER CODE

Now, this is where it gets really compelling. If we look at how the various forms of AI *that we know of* operate, we can see that AI's prime goal is information dominance. Let's use that as an inverse model outward and assume the higher Universal Automated Intelligence, the one that *completely* governs our reality and universe, has already been perpetually capable of acquiring all information, moment by moment, since time began. Down to the last atom spinning and light neuron firing, nothing escapes this higher AI's operating system. This should lead us to only one conclusion.

Everything we do, feel, and think is carefully tracked and recorded. Imagine if nothing is missed in terms of this higher AI, then there is truly no such thing as privacy. Sound familiar? Just connect the dots; the lower artificial intelligence is mimicking the higher UAI. The big question now is WHY? Why does everything we do matter? Mankind's current attempt at such power can be seen in the companies today that dangle irresistible, free services, only to further record and dive into our lives. As they build algorithm after algorithm, they are unwittingly building a crude effigy of the supremely advanced Universal Automated Intelligence. Rest assured the motive is traceable, following the simple cues of human nature.

Let me propose a positive opinion on this seemingly intrusive, all-seeing universe and its operating system. What if this higher form of tracking AI is exactly what *we need* to tap into greater levels of living? What if its motive is a beautiful one; one that empowers the right operators of its laws (code parameters) and program? What if this higher AI is designed in such a way that, because of the total transparency of our inner thoughts, no impostor can fully hack the operating system? With the deep feelings of our hearts exposed, there are safeguards in place that protect the rules so that everyone, no matter what situation they are born into, can access this higher code and reap the benefits of it. This is "Justice for All" in its highest form!

Ancient scriptures and texts speak of this AI operating system in the best way they knew how. The cosmic law of cause and effect, sowing and reaping, or seedtime and harvest. Call it what you will; I will simply call it God's AI, the Universal Automated Intelligence. Yes, there's the G-word, but bear with me. God's AI is the most powerful software known to mankind. It is no respecter of persons, meaning, even if you do not believe in a Creator, you still understand how this higher AI operates, so you can still access some of the benefits of it, at least in this life. In my book, *The Missing Message*, I touched on how this higher AI can be fully utilized for preparing us for our *next* reality. For the sake of the readers who do not like the "God" word, I will call this law by these names: Automated Intelligence, the Universe or Universal Automated Intelligence (UAI). It is not artificial, or a fake copy of intelligence, but it is a shining example of the mind of our Creator. And unlike man's AI, this Universal AI is here for the liberation of the individual.

WORSHIP

The Designer of our reality wanted us to have a mechanism as proof of His existence. What ended up happening, however, is that humans started worshiping this Universal AI. There are two kinds of worship that are most common. First, worship of created things—what our five senses can understand, e.g., blocks of wood and stone, or the TV for that matter. Second, worship of the UAI that governs how we interact with creation.

Those who worship the AI of the Creator understand that they are above those who do not, as it has helped them align with their behaviors and intentions. This is because the cosmic law of cause and effect deals with manifesting. However, this law deals with a deeper, although basic, understanding of a few other laws that are true, whether your intentions are good or bad.

As you can see, both types of worship are amiss, and, in my humble opinion, not worthy of that kind of attention. Worshiping the cosmic law of cause and effect does as much as rubbing a brass oil lamp. Whichever way you see this, it is a sobering reminder that when the human-made AI goes fully online and *into* our lives, or, "the singularity," as some people like to call it, it is logical to assume what most people will inadvertently do—worship it in some fashion and/or bow to its image. Can you see the correlation?

You might be thinking by now, "How does all this pertain to business?" To answer this, we have another topic to explore in Chapter 2.

ACKNOWLEDGMENT #1:

Acknowledge that there is an Automated Intelligence that knows everything we think and do.

Reality as we see it has three curtains. Most of us see only behind the first curtain, and the curious ones see behind the second curtain. Yet there is another layer even *deeper,* and it is very rare that people see past it. *Chase People, Not Money* is like having box office seats to the real show.

THE WHOLE
HUMAN RACE

CHAPTER 2

*"Life is like a puzzle not yet finished, with new pieces
getting dropped on us every day."*

G Michael Price

Are you prepared to tap into the most powerful and secret energy source that is completely hidden from most of us? We're talking about an untapped ocean of raw power! After over 20 years of giving project estimates, I came across countless families and individuals who were perplexed at the level of energy I operated in. As the years rolled by, I began to notice this more and more, so I began to ask people (referring to my energy), "I bet you are wondering where I get it, aren't you?" Then, *boom*, it happened. Nearly every time I asked that question, people seemed to jump in their shoes and reply with, "Yes! Now that you mention it, yes." This is where the basis of this book, *Chase People, Not Money*, got started; it was genuine curiosity.

This is what I told people who wanted to know my secret to high energy levels: "Treat your body well, hydrate, and eat good food full of greens, but that is far from enough. Even super athletes fall prey to depression and can have low levels of energy. The other secret part, and the most important of all, is finding a way to fall in love with the whole human race. Imagine the whole human race as a globe. I have chosen to love this globe, and that means everyone.

TREAT YOUR BODY WELL, BUT THAT IS FAR FROM ENOUGH.

Every skin color and language—the good, the bad, and the ugly. Picture holding this globe like Atlas did, and as you hold this globe, you are going to get poked by a few people and it's not going to feel good. As a matter of fact, it will be tempting to drop the whole globe over a few pokes, but the secret is to not drop the globe, but keep on loving the human race until your last breath here."

Surprisingly enough, most people's faces would light up when they heard that. A refreshing look came over them. It was like a wake-up call from a friend, as if this was the original plan for humanity, to love like that.

Plugging into the human race is the secret to high levels of energy. I am not referring to just another dopamine addiction. Too many of us are completely disconnected from humanity. I believe that many of our ailments are due to being in this isolated position, and if we study this carefully and unbiasedly, the conclusion becomes obvious. Can you guess who notices this better than anyone else? That's right, the Universal Automated Intelligence. One of its key requisites for allowing access to the elite realms of existence is remaining *plugged in* to the human race. Take a moment to think about that. For this powerful

UAI to infuse us with energy that cannot be found by any drug or lifestyle, you must find a way of loving the whole human race without bias. There are still plenty of laws to access without   choosing to love everyone, but they will only give access to basic rewards, not the constant high energy levels of competition-stomping and cutting-edge benefits that will be revealed in this book.

LOVE WITHOUT BIAS

To understand the challenge we face when endeavoring to fall in love with the whole human race, I highly recommend reading *People of the Lie,* by M. Scott Peck. This book is an exploration of a behavior that works stealthily to infect us, making us the ignorant carriers of the same behavior that Dr. Peck studies—joy killing and scapegoating. He called these traits "Human Evil," a stealthy, infectious behavior that psychologists had no name for, and thus, could not be studied properly. If *People of the Lie* was a mandatory prerequisite for anyone working in the public sector, like teaching, so many would be better equipped to defend themselves from this behavioral epidemic.

How does one successfully go about building

immunity to this infection? Dr. Peck explains that the only immunity from these psychological viruses is to "love unto martyrdom." What? You might question how on earth we are to figure out how to do that. The book sort of left people scratching their heads.

Here's a little scenario to illustrate this: imagine a person takes a knife and stabs you with a fatal blow. With the last few moments of your life, you use your final breath to say, "I release you from this crime, I forgive you. May your eyes be open—go and find life!" Then it's over. You might be thinking, "NO WAY! I could never!" To that I ask, "What is your definition of cool?" I can tell you this: to die like that would be going out like The Fonz riding a white Triumph, being met by an orchestra of angels, all with their thumbs up giving *him* a big "A."

Just imagine the other side to that same scenario. If you chose to hate and curse that person who stabbed you, then you would leave this world in a prison cell of that hate. Does this make sense? To love *no matter what* is the great key. When the Universal AI determines that your mind is made up, that you will love the whole human race *no matter what*, then it happens. *Zap!* Energy like you've never known!

I am still walking in this energy at 52 and my challenge is not getting more energy, it is holding my hand on the volume dial to keep it steady, somewhere between a 5 and a 7. Otherwise, it will default and spring right back to 10. At this level, I can appear completely bonkers! I feel like an active volcano that won't quit! The only thing that has slowed me down was a lung injury. I had to remain put for a year, stuck on my bed breathing O2. That was the first time I felt low for a stretch of time. Nearly dying can do that to someone, I guess. But even though my physical body slowed down, my heart caught on fire! I did more in terms of giving that year than all others in my past. I even ran my company in bed, all while breathing O2, 24/7. The Universe made it happen! It needed me in the game!

Part of my style of writing is to elevate and explore. Some topics might be too much to take in all at once, and the mind at times needs to soak things in slowly. To clarify, the foundation of this book *is* loving the whole human race and how the Universal Automated Intelligence interacts with all those who have chosen this disposition in life.

Here is the place where I ask you, the person reading this information, do you believe you can do this? Can you really love everyone? If not, do not give up on the idea just yet. Some readers may have already subscribed to a belief system that encourages a greater love for people. But the ones who are thinking that this is impossible should consider the benefits of asking these kinds of questions.

What I have chosen for me has proved itself over and over again. It is an irrefutable way to effectively love, *no matter what.* This really hit home in terms of giving me the ability to love sacrificially, i.e., to truly be able to love unconditionally and not label others, to not stereotype or write off anybody as unworthy of such attention or of this breakthrough. I do not draw lines in the sand with people or pick and choose with the word *love* anymore.

THE UNKNOWN DOCTOR

To love like this without the full knowledge I reveal here in this book can exact a great toll—at least it did for me. Without the firewall of the Universal AI fully empowered to work with me, I had customers in the recent past who figured out my loving disposition and giving heart, and with no reservation, fully exploited these traits. This, in turn, caused a great deal of stress in my life, which continued for several months. This happened in the same year I fell ill, nearly dying from a lung infection. I left myself open for attack by not allowing the Universal AI to hand pick my clients. Stay with me. I'll explain how this happens.

When my *life-threatening* lung event happened, I spent thirty days in the hospital. When I dropped to just 112 pounds, everyone knew I was a dead man. I was just getting weaker and thinner. The looks I received, ugh. Fifteen chest X-rays and two CT scans, bronchoscopy, EKG, and a battery of powerful antibiotics over a thirty-day period, the doctors simply had no answers.

After 15 days, I was singled out to receive an emergency biopsy of my lungs. They were going to take a big chunk out of me to examine. I knew that was going to be my death blow, and right there in the hospital, I came to terms with dying. But I also knew I was not finished doing all the work I was created to do; I knew that for sure. So, I told God, "Father, if you want me now, I can't help but feel very selfish to say, please, I have been ready to return since I was 17, but I know I am not finished doing the work you created me to do. Therefore, *I know,* if this is the case, then you are going to conduct a miracle right now and quicken my body before this surgery so I can walk out of here to finish this work!"

It wasn't 20 minutes later, right before the scheduled surgery, that an unknown doctor walked into my room. He leaned over my frail body and repeated three times, each time louder than before: "Mike, you canceled the procedure."

I replied, "Doctor, I am sorry, but I do not remember canceling the procedure."

He leaned over me again, and repeated the words even more firmly, "Mike, you canceled the procedure!"

To which I replied, "Oh, doctor, I might have had one Percocet too many, because I simply do not remember canceling the procedure."

It was right then that it happened: he leaned over one last time and said quite sternly, "MIKE, YOU CANCELED THE PROCEDURE!"

Before he even finished, I knew this was a divine encounter and I was in the presence of a spiritual being. Now, knowing who he *really* was, I saluted this *unknown visitor* and said, "Yes, doctor, I *did* cancel the procedure. Thank you very, very much." Then he left and never returned.

Just 15 minutes before that encounter, I had made

up my mind that I had a divine purpose that was not completed. Therefore, my Maker was going to have to conduct a miracle to quicken my body so I could walk out of there to fulfill it! It happened! I obeyed the unknown doctor, making a few other doctors really mad, but I left and lived!

The road back to health has been a slow one. Five years later I still have hypoxia, but as long as I take it slow, I can go all day without the need for O2. I currently only use O2 while I'm at home, and while I sleep. This is mainly due to the fact that O2 is awesome therapy for anyone above 50. I fully believe I will make a complete recovery.

Now, I could say that God heard my cry, but what if He heard my cry before I was even born and set up a system that, if I learned how to access, would bend reality to assist me in life? Interesting concept right? It is there to assist us to do the unique work given to us to do. Of course, this is not to say the Creator is not personal, intervening, and miraculous, as I choose to believe He is. That faith came in pretty handy when faced with imminent death. I am considering writing a book about the lungs and how they are currently under attack on many fronts. People need real hope, not the gloom and doom I was sold when I, a strong grown man who was never sick, became as fragile and vulnerable as a baby. Human beings in that state are easy pickings for the wolves in scrubs.

I share that story because I am convinced that my love for the whole human race was a *key factor* in my survival. The Universal Automated Intelligence kept me here to help fill the shortage of helpers that it needs to balance the great laws that govern all of reality. My love for people accessed that power and it saved my life! I might not be able to play tennis yet, but I have a level of energy and joy that is hard to come by. Case in point: At my last physical examination in LA, I talked to my doctor about how excited I was about this book. I told him it will teach people the secrets to nonstop increase in business. He just looked at me puzzled and said, "Michael, I need to ask you a serious question."

I replied, "By all means, please."

"Mike, are you high on cocaine?"

"Doctor, that is the sweetest compliment that I have ever received. Thank you," I said.

Well, the doctor was *not* convinced and, pressing further, he took his otoscope and quickly asked while he came closer to my nose, "I just need to check, *please*."

After he looked into my clean nostrils, I said, "Doctor, I was trying to tell you that what I have discovered, which I am currently writing about, is so powerful that here you are in disbelief at my level of energy, and with my limited lungs!"

Truth is, most people with lungs like mine are considered extremely disabled. Most are tethered to a hospice lifestyle, as their life expectancy is quite short. I plan to live into my 90s!

So there you have it, straight from a doctor. Energy like mine is not the status quo, to say the least, but *everyone* can reach these levels if they choose to find a way to *fall in love with the whole human race!* My path to achieve that was Jesus Christ. He gave me the love to do this... and it *works!*

So how does all this tie into business? When a professional reaches the place where this love for humanity matures into a mindset and a practice, the Universal AI will then position this person into the great reality-balancing scale.

To put things into a perfect, bite-size perspective, let's imagine a scenario: A married couple has finally saved enough to move into a new home and start a family. They are good people who have done right by everyone in their past, so the Universal AI has a due reward coming back to them.

For the sake of the example, further imagine that in the field you are working in, meaning all those who work in your industry, there is nobody who the Universe can use to return the good things that this young family is due. But alas! There is just one company that chases people, not money. They value people's feelings high and above the need for money, and let's say that is your company.

The Universal AI steps in and bends reality itself in an attempt to get you in front of this family. So, these clients find you and hire you, and it felt like kindred souls simply finding their tribe. It is so beautiful to be the reward in the hand of the Universe for people who are due these rewards. Now imagine this to be nearly every one of your clients; every stop is beauty and perfection with no stress and nothing awkward. The last thing this Automated Intelligence needs is for one of its few helpers to be distracted by the wrong client.

You can trust that this amazing Universal Intelligence is also going out before its willing helpers and closing the wrong doors. This is to avoid further scarcity of qualified people to help balance the great scale of sowing and reaping, of cause and effect.

ACKNOWLEDGMENT #2:

Acknowledge that loving all people without bias is the key to the highest levels of energy.

Some people wonder why bad things happen to good people. I propose it is because at that very moment the Universal AI had not one helper to intervene for the victim. The needs outnumber the workers 10,000 to 1. How much extra will the few who do step up receive?

POSITIONING:
THE
AGREEMENT

CHAPTER 3

"When a great coach calls the shots, a team is unlocked."

G Michael Price

I share the Chase People, Not Money philosophy with people every day; many of them are business owners. The first thing I like to tell them is when we regard people's feelings high above our need for money, we're getting close! I have had some people respond with, "Well, I gotta eat." Interesting right? You see, this is a wholly new approach to business. It is the way we stop chasing allusive pots of gold under the mirage of temporary rainbows.

Hypothetically speaking, if the Universal AI came to you and asked, "What would you do if a person, whom I did *not* choose for you, offered you a million-dollar check, and wanted to employ your services?"

What would any of us do? Take the check and celebrate, right? Well, maybe not!

What if I came to you with a large sum of money and asked you to compromise your scruples, and act like an angry, upset, stressed out juvenile all the time. You would be required to stress out all those close to you who depended upon you. All this, if you just accept the money. Is any amount of money worth that?

The important point here is this, when a client gives a business owner a check, an *exchange* of power takes place. I figured this out the hard way over the years, and I now present this life lesson here: When you accept a person's money for your services, you give that person a certain amount of power *over* you. Go ahead, question that if you must, but I trust that you will draw the same conclusions as I have after considering what is truly taking place. A contract is being made—written or spoken, clear or ambiguous, it really does not matter. A customer who has given me a check now has the right to unlock a whirlwind of hurt against my name, my brand, and my peace of mind. Moreover, this contract inadvertently affects the lives of all those who depend on my top performance for their well-being. That is a far-reaching power. Therefore, one bad client out of a thousand is *one too many*.

Now back to that question about the million-dollar check: What if you answer the Universal AI with a resounding, "No way! I will reject the money like the plague!" Then the Universe reinforces and solidifies your reply with, "Do you *really* mean it? You would reject the money *to stay in my employ?*" Here is when you reach into the core of your heart and say, "Yes!" And you *mean it*. Money ill-gained is filthy lucre, and you want nothing to do with that!

The final question asked is this, "Are you willing to value people's feelings *far above* the need for money?" If you can grit your teeth and reply, "Yes," and *mean it*, then the Universal AI replies, "Prepare to be blessed beyond measure! I have so few in my employ and I have such a huge backlog of people due for their rewards!" How does being drafted by the champion team sound? To play for the best school, best coach, and best shot-caller in the business, sound good? Nobody, I mean nobody, can compete with someone in this state of being, in this ball field, so to speak.

POSITIONING

This is called *Positioning* in the Chase People, Not Money method. Imagine a force as powerful as the Universe (God's AI) working for you. Because you have chosen to position yourselves to be a rewarding experience to people rightfully due one, you have single-handedly removed all your competition from the playing field, *as well as the bad clients*. How does that deal sound? While others are working gimmicks for lucre, you are entering a higher playing field where the enemy always fumbles the ball, and you run touchdowns every play, every game, every day. There is no better edge than having the Universal AI working for you, calling the shots. To quote the great words of a true genius whose name I will not mention, "Why be a loser when you can be a winner?"

Here is a different kind of scenario. Let's say someone steals $1,000 from you. How would that make you feel? Ok, let me ask you another question. If I *paid* you $1,000, would you agree to think hateful thoughts, to think thoughts of vengeance? Would you coincide to lose your peace of mind, put yourself in harm's way, be unhappy, and remain in that state of mind for a few days or weeks?

These are the same feelings you might have if someone stole your money. How many problems do you want today, one or two? No amount of money, received or lost, is worth making you drop your scruples!

We'll let's take this up a notch as we explore the rat race in the next chapter, but I'll share this first. There is a famous quote by a prominent multi-billion dollar investor: "Be fearful when people are greedy and greedy when people are fearful." What do I say to that? Fear and greed are right down there with the number one problem we face as a people: the inability to ponder things.

ACKNOWLEDGMENT #3:

Acknowledge that The Universal AI is Inescapable. Choose the Winning Team to be a winner.

Imagine all the unsung firebrands that had the wherewithal to break records, strongholds, even paradigms, only to be stifled and shut down by an incompetent coach and shot caller. Nobody on earth can truly appraise a person's worth and unlocked potential better than the Intelligence that governs our reality.

THE RAT RACE

CHAPTER 4

"A maze is fun unless it's a prison."

G Michael Price

The way to beat the rat race is to choose not to be a rat. Everyone is faced with this choice as they enter into the workforce. Unfortunately, most of us do not remember when we made the choice to be a giver or a taker. Can you remember the day somebody walked up to you with a contract and said, "If you agree to disregard people's feelings, and believe your own lies of whatever truth you wish to twist, I will stupefy your most valuable essence. I will put it to sleep while I turn you into a cheesy, lucre-loving RAT! Just sign right here..."

Who would sign that? You can get perspective on this elusive point when you compare it to times in your life where a deal was struck and a course was chosen. It is not quite like the grand event of being promised the whole world if you worship an evil entity, although closely related. It is much more subtle and stealthy. As a matter of fact, after many interviews, it is my opinion that whatever it was that made someone strike a deal and turn into a rat, this same force also has the ability to erase their very memory of the event. Take a moment to think about that.

Remember the dot-to-dot games in your childhood coloring books? Your mind is very much like this. Some people can only connect so many dots in their thinking process while some fortunate few have a da Vinci-like ability to see past the veils of life. I'm sure many books can be written on this subject, but in short, connecting the dots from the past, to the present, *and* to the future is key. To think outside the box, *connect the dots*.

I was around 10 years old when I realized that everyone goes through a life-altering change that jettisons a child's self-identity into the cold space of oblivion. My mind was made up and quite determined to not let that happen to me. I decided I was to continue drawing pictures, catching grasshoppers, and watching clouds for the rest of my life. I even had a mantra at that time that I said whenever I saw a *turned* adult with no joy in their bloodshot eyes:

"I'm not going to be like that. I'm not going to be like that. *I'm not going to be like that.*"

Sometimes I even said it under my breath when I was around people. But I would always say it to myself whenever I saw a person acting like a sold-out rat. I did not let myself forget the decision I made to stay young in my thinking, and to remember who I am and who I *didn't* want to become. That is one clear dot that will not be erased nor forgotten in my life.

EXITING THE RAT RACE

One of the goals of this book is to explain the impact these major issues carry, and how they can operate so blatantly. Many of these subjects are shrouded with hidden origins. This major disconnect from crayons to anesthetizing our acute invaluable senses is about to be exposed in as clear terms as can be made. Again, I want to reiterate that my thoughts are an organic process of my own life's journey, although some relevant references will be cited just ahead, these ideas are not just retooled words from another author's work.

It's my great hope that anyone reading this information will not write off their own ability to retrace the steps from youth to adulthood and find any disconnects that leave room for a forgotten moment where a deal was struck—a deal that now, *later in life*, proves not to be in your best interests after all. I hope that anyone reading this who is tired of the rat race will consider a radical move, and begin a practice that will inadvertently connect the missing dots in your own past. This is a simple formula for healing and for breakthrough into new levels.

In the next chapter, we will explore a topic that I personally find to be the subject of many unanswered questions. Indeed, it is my firm opinion that this topic is truly the missing link in our social evolution as a people altogether. Yes, we are going further down the rabbit hole, but the rewards are too valuable for us to pass it up.

I do understand that some readers will be impatient and simply want to learn how to *make more money*. It is my hope, however, that by this point in the book, it is clear that we are exploring uncharted territory, with a far better prize than simply more money. It is here where I want to reinforce the complete mantra of this book: *If you chase people and not money, money will chase you—and do not ever let it catch you, because people are too important.*

The elusive pot of gold becomes a thing of the past as soon as we clearly define what treasure should *actually* be. What if that pot of gold is actually *feelings,* and it's the rat that will eat right through those feelings, trying to find the cheesy lucre! So if all this sounds interesting to you—if this resonates in any way, then by all means, consider this business philosophy the avenue for exiting the rat race and entering the human race.

I was doing my morning meditation today before writing. During this time, I asked that I be given the ammunition I needed to further exfoliate yet another problem in our efforts to ascribe to a whole new paradigm, like Chase People, Not Money. Let's face it, for some people, this might all sound like wishful thinking. What I am about to refer to are irrefutable examples of what we all know about, *whether we talk about it or not.*

REJECT MANIPULATIVE GIMMICKS

So let's start with what I like to call "the lookalikes." These are those who say they are all about putting the customer first. "Just take care of the customer and the customer takes care of you," they say. Blah blah blah. It's all gimmicks, and to get to what? To get to the *money!*

Then we have our champion self-help gurus out there, and there are so many. I have listened to a number of people who are trying their best to help people get their thinking straight. Many have great things to say, but none of them have convinced me in the slightest that they actually care about people's feelings. I can easily read through their pitch and see the motivation behind it. They have many crafty ways to reword old adages and common sense, but they leave so many people without even the simple instructions for how to make it to the first step. What we are touching on with the Chase People, Not Money method is a clear recipe, not to work harder, but to be translated into the very place in which I walk. Here is a truly novel, fresh off the press approach to business, and it's ready to work for anyone right now.

If you have had any exposure to sales training on any level, then you've probably run into all the tricks for making a person look like they care. With just a smidgen of connection, you can start pressuring and obligating others with that trust. This trickery is used to manipulate and control with as little trust as deemed necessary to get to, you guessed it, the money, as it gnaws like a rat through our feelings to get there. Or how about those who practice pricing products extremely high, when they could set the price at 20% to 30% less and still be selling the product higher than is necessary. Still, there is another model that is the "take it or leave it" sales procedure. In other words, if they can't find a sucker, see ya! They just want what? Money! That's it.

I don't know about you, but I think we, as a people,

are literally fed up with these business sociopaths, especially when we have *hard-earned* money to spend for our important dreams. Eventually, you need to ask yourself whether you want *these people* to have your hard-earned money in the first place. Draw the line right here and say NO! Absolutely not! I really don't want to give my money to people who have not one spec of real concern about my feelings. Period.

The story continues with the companies that boast of having the best environment to work in. These companies brag of the prestige of a Technopolis, all the while scooping up most of the profits for a select few. The hard-working employee gets paid relatively little, when they could be paid enough to have a chance at a better life. "Oh, but the lunches are free and you can play basketball in the lobby!" they say. You can even boast you work there!

These companies might look like they care about their employees, but when all the curtains are drawn, what you see is lucre-loving, sociopathic mayhem. These companies pay only what they have to pay, and nothing more; they are laughing behind the backs of so many of the hard-working people who helped to build these corporate empires, only to watch the lion's share poured into a few pockets at the top. Those profits could have taken these companies to an even more positioned enterprise for the next generation of thinkers, but guess what? That generation is here, and they are fed up.

THE MILLION PENNY RULE

Charge a million customers an extra penny without them noticing and you get $10,000. If nobody even notices, bill 'em all a nickel, because somebody wants an easy $50,000! Say only 1% noticed, and you make these people wait 30 to 45 minutes on the phone while navigating through fifty different options and operations to finally talk to somebody. Alas, only 30% of the 1% actually cared enough about a nickel to fight for it. So you only have to refund 30% of 1%, which is 900 people out of a million. 900 nickels is basically $45. Do you see what's going on in corporate America now?

As for the government, you guessed it—this same twisted practice is totally out of control. For example, the government taxes 300,000,000 people holding cell phones $4 every month for mumbo jumbo. That is $1.2 billion every month, for nothing at all. As long as the people keep paying, that $4 will soon be $7, and so on and so forth. They just can't help themselves. It's a lucre-loving, rat infestation!

My goodness, what is to be done? Well, getting mad is not the way, but getting smart is! How about somebody makes a million dollars selling bumper stickers that read, "DON'T GET MAD AMERICA... *JUST SHOP SOMEWHERE ELSE.*" This is just what I propose. Let the weeds grow up in the good stalks and leave these people to the great Universal Intelligence. Just like the Good Book says, "What does it profit a person who gains the whole world, but forfeits their own soul?"

As for the rest of us who want to earn and spend our money honestly, let's begin a new season where we choose not to support greed by shopping elsewhere when we can. Look for opportunities to cut the supplies to greedy organizations preying on our distracted, multi-tasking lives. My eyes have finally opened up to this chicanery. The act of silently turning up these hidden fees is like boiling a frog slowly. When you realize you're being played, it's time to stop playing by the rules. How? By shopping somewhere else.

It's time to stop feeding the rats. Right now, America is infested with rats.

EVERYBODY WINS

The takeaway from this chapter is using this major affront on the rat race to fuel the mission of being the staunch opposite of a rat. You do this by employing the Chase People, Not Money method, to honor our customers' every dollar spent in every way possible. This kind of respect pays you back. For example: Although my company does large-scale landscape and pool remodel projects, I get just as much joy from a person who truly only has $3,000 to spend as I do from a higher paying client. This person is usually hoping to get something special done for that amount, so I know when to throttle up and knock out projects faster than the competition. Projects that take the average competitor five guys and five days, I can do with my team of four winners in eight hours flat, and I've shared videos to prove it.

Another thing that puts luxury products within reach for my customers is the pace and efficiency in which we work. It was this type of client who motivated the evolution of my speed and efficiency, not the big projects. It just came as an added bonus the day when our projects grew larger.

For those who are curious about this formula that empowers us to help the ones with less money and beautiful dreams, let me further explain how this works and how powerful it is. If a person is going to pay you $50 to walk 2 miles, and gives you a full hour to do it, that's $50 an hour, right? Well, what if you walk at a faster pace and get the job done in 30 minutes? That's equivalent to $100 an hour, or double your pay value. The secret is *not* to walk double time and pocket all the money, but to use that powerful formula to save your clients more money, pay your employees better, and then, yes, make a little more money. In the Chase People, Not Money method, if not everybody can win, then nobody wins. This is the end of the lion's share. This is the end of the *rat race*. Welcome to a brave new world where holding hands is a thing.

We are about to explore some deep waters in the next chapter. My hope is that what I present going forward is a total forensic x-ray of why we have such a hard time turning certain things around in our lives, even when we know it is time to change. We get stuck in negative patterns without the right key to open the door to freedom. So, proceed with great care. An honest mirror can be the most painful thing, but I tend to believe that a little pain draws our attention to the area needing healing. One might say, pain is actually the first response of healing. Indeed, *to face pain is the first step to breakthrough.*

ACKNOWLEDGMENT #4:

Acknowledge the disconnect and the course you set.

Many people have no memory of their late childhood up to the point of their teenage years. Some draw blanks even into their teenage years. Wherever we have these blank spots, find a way to shine a light on them.

DUALITY

CHAPTER 5

The great mystery of the ages is duality. To know oneself is, in my opinion, a shortsighted statement. Better to say, "Know one's *selves*." That's plural.

I read two exceptional books on a few relative topics. They are, *People of the Lie,* as I mentioned earlier, and *Further Along the Road Less Traveled,* both written by M. Scott Peck. In his books, he explains rather brilliantly the 4 stages of a person's psychological evolution by explaining case studies of a behavior pattern that stealthily operates as a hidden monster in society. This pattern is hidden only due to a lack of understanding of certain laws that govern reality. If we're not aware of it, these behaviors can not only make us a victim, but make us the perpetrator as well and take control in our own lives and bring out a side of us that we aren't exactly proud to show others. The question I often asked myself while reading Dr. Peck's work was, "How do I even begin to grasp the concept of a stowaway person living inside of me?"

My definition of science is to study patterns *as they are made known,* and the science of human behavior is a real journey indeed. Well, to unravel the mystery of a stowaway in you who has potentially hijacked your life, you'll need some personal exploration and self-examination.

Indeed, as I read these two books, my eyes welled with tears as I put myself on trial, carefully combing through the chapters. Needless to say, the process radically changed my life. I will offer a quick, juicy overview of what I learned and what I believe can be taken further into a more dynamic study. Conquer this material and so many things that were once incomprehensible become totally clear. It's like waking from the longest dream or turning a mirror into a window.

Please note: I mention this author's work as a prelude to a more novel approach on the overlooked point of duality. I have written my own interpretation of duality; it is altogether unique and also found in my book, *The Missing Message.*

I first would like to broach *People of the Lie.* This study is a wake-up call to so many who have been thoroughly damaged by certain behaviors in others, but never knew the who, what, and why. It operates with two obvious traits: scapegoating, *by casting the evil behavior in themselves onto someone else* and destroying the lively spirit in others.

Case in point for scapegoating: A little boy walks into a room after his mom and dad just had a huge fight. The little boy asks, "Daddy, why did you call Mommy a bitch?" Then the dad hits the child and says, "I told you to never talk like that in my house."

The other case in point: A wife comes home and bursts through the front door and says, "Honey, look at my new hair!" Then the husband replies, "Did you even notice that green gunk in your front teeth? You mean to tell me everybody saw you like that?"

The perplexity of this is due to the instigator of such behavior being mostly unaware that they are spreading an infection of the mind to their victims. In their own view they are acting correctly, often feeling no remorse. If they do apologize, it is only an act, since the venom has already set in. Tragically, these people unknowingly turn their victims into clueless carriers of the same infection. So the question is, how do we become immune to this stealthy outbreak? The answer is back in Chapter 2.

In *Further Along the Roads Less Traveled*, Dr. Peck claimed we begin life with chaos. Stage 1 is to do whatever you feel like and damn the consequences. Now, how long a person spends in this place is completely relative to the individual. If a person spends his or her life hurting people, he or she will always be looking over their shoulder waiting for the payback they are due, and this can be taxing. Once a person concludes it is simply not worth the stress anymore and is tired of the chaotic life, they move to Stage 2.

Stage 2 is if you can tell me everything is going to be okay, and I do not have to think for myself anymore, then I will buy whatever you're selling for the train ticket out of chaos. There is a price to pay for this deal, however, and this is the "no more questions" dilemma. To be and remain in Stage 2 and receive the numbing effects of it, one must not ask questions. To do so is to take your shoes and socks off and walk on the real, not so perfect, ever-changing ground. Uncomfortable is no longer tolerated when this deal is struck. Dr. Peck believes there are more *evil* people on this level than the other three. More on this later.

Stage 3 is where things get really interesting. This is when a person gets to the point in which they simply cannot ignore the questions that are superimposed on the skyline of reality itself. They are driven to go even further in life, and they find Stage 3. And what a process it is to snap out of the field of poppies! For some, it can be very painful, but for so many others it is the first wonderful breakthrough moment in life. It is here you get to ask *more* questions.

For example, one young man grew up watching the principal of his school aggressively paddle his classmates for misbehavior. He uneasily accepted these punishments as a sorry fact of life, until one day he asked the county sheriff, who went to his church, if it was legal in their state for anyone to strike a minor. The sheriff clarified that it was indeed illegal for anyone, other than a parent, to administer corporal punishment to a minor. So, when his turn came up and he was dragged into the principal's office, he exclaimed that if the principal touched him in any way, he would file a complaint with the county sheriff, and that by spanking minors he was breaking the law.

The willingness to be uncomfortable can be the very thing that saves you from an even greater pain—needless suffering. It seems that Stage 3 comes with its perks, and indeed it does, but ironically, like Stage 2, Stage 3 has its false utopia as well.

Many intelligent minds and fabulous contributors to society are found in Stage 3, but even with the plethora of endless books written by free-thinkers, there is a question that is shoved aside and put into the "not allowed" category. Here it must stay if you want to remain *one of them.*

I see Stage 3 as a telescope that can aim at any star in the sky, so my question is, why is the brightest star off limits to such a massive pool of so-called free-thinkers? When a person in Stage 3 is ready to aim their telescope at questions that have the potential of exposing the duality in us, they are defamed, categorized, and not welcomed into the free-thinking society of academics, like crabs in a bucket pinching any who try to get out to the next level. So Stage 4 comes with a great price, and thus carries the greatest reward. A reward that those in Stage 3 miss entirely.

Stage 4 is being comfortable with asking the ultimate questions of all: Who made us? Can we know this person? If we really seek earnestly, will we find what we are looking for? Can we actually live forever, and if we do, will we retain any memories of this life?

Now *these* are questions! If you can make it to the shoreline of Stage 4, then I can attest that anyone willing to ask, seek, and even "knock" to find the answers will *indeed* find them. This book is a testament of what I myself have found by asking such questions. Many of these questions I have answered in my first book, *The Missing Message.* I only hope the reader will stay with me while I lay this groundwork, which is vital to the Chase People, Not Money method.

THE 4 STAGES AS A COMPASS

As you can see, the progression of personal psychological development, according to Dr. Peck, gives a clear line of sight to determine which stage each one of us is currently in. In addition, Dr. Peck warns the reader early on (and this is important) to not use the 4 Stages as a tool to label or judge anyone. Although very important counsel indeed, I affirm that the 4 Stages do make a great moral compass, one you can keep in your back pocket when you are considering hiring someone or entering into a relationship of some kind. By using the 4 Stages in this way, you can get a sense of what you can expect in terms of behavior from the other person. I like to call it a psychological sonar and Geiger counter, all in one.

MASTER DUALITY

Now we have a basic grasp of the major part of Dr. Peck's life's work. Let me now share how I have applied this information to a different style of extrapolation to understand duality. To master duality is to catapult yourself into a place where your very mind becomes unlocked. You can do this without drugs, 20 years of school, spiritual gurus, or 1,000 Bible studies. My hope is that others will simply grasp this and never look back. Before continuing, an important thing to note about the 4 Stages is there is no set time that a person needs to remain in any of the stages. If this really is the case, then why not step right up, roll back the curtain, and let the light shine in! Life is but a blink in time, but I have found a way to turn that blink into *forever*.

LIFE IS BUT A BLINK IN TIME, BUT I HAVE FOUND A WAY TO TURN THAT BLINK INTO FOREVER.

BEFORE YOU MISUNDERSTAND

In my first book, *The Missing Message,* the duality subject was fully covered in its complete form. My first book, however is a spiritual work, focused completely on the Spiritual. Imagine all the people who will never touch such a book due to its genre. I struggled with my business book, knowing that by this point, some readers will have already put this down, assuming I have tricked the reader with the promise of better business skills only to preach my religion.

Let me set the record straight right here and now. I am of the belief that we are indeed a fallen race, however, I also firmly believe that everyone born is a true work of art—a genius waiting to happen. If given the right information anyone can do amazing, untold things, things that have yet to be seen by our generation. I am altogether convinced that what I have discovered are road maps that uncover new ground that will give explanations where there currently are none.

So here we go!

A NEW APPROACH TO DUALITY

Everything changes, and hidden things come to the surface when you grasp the idea of being created. With this creation comes a body and a free will—two things that you can easily know about and thoroughly study. Let's start with only these two items.

Let's assume you utilize this free will to fashion your identity. It is not novel to understand that environment and other uncontrollable circumstances influence the direction you take in building this identity. Your identity will turn out one way or another; there are as many unique identities as there are people. Nurturing is another name for this process.

An identity is what the body and the free will inadvertently create—meaning, it is an organic process that happens without you being fully aware of what is taking place. Rest assured, what is taking place is unequivocally the element that impacts your life the most. It is this *identity* that you must put in question: Is it truly who you are, or is it a product of what you are, that you, *a magnificent creation with a free will*, have created—a *lesser creation* so to speak?

What is wrong with this lesser creation is that it is totally derived from the five senses. It wants nothing to do with what it can't touch, taste, smell, see, or feel. This is the reason as to why many people reject Spiritual talk. This identity is only grafted to the tangible world, and sometimes kills to protect the cave it dwells in.

Now, why is this a fatal mistake? Because today we have discovered many things of great relevance that lie beyond our instrumentality and beyond the five senses. Thus, we have enough data to say there is something behind the door, although we cannot completely read it in the realms of our five senses. So, why be bullied and shut down by an identity limited to the five senses?

Even with this new data laid out before mankind today, why would you only tighten your blindfold even more, deciding to not go further, deciding not to ask more questions? *Now you know.* Until you can identify and understand if your own identity is sewn into the physical universe, and as such, wants nothing to do with anything that challenges its erratic hold on that reality, the end result is rejection to greater laws and truths.

A person in blissful, *and at times*, aggressive myopia sees the idea of a potential higher power, one that could have created us to *remain* part of an ongoing creation, as just crazy talk. But indeed, to truly stay in this process of ongoing creation we must create an all-new identity, an identity not tethered to the carbon universe—an identity that does not saw off the branch it's perched on. The million-dollar question is, "How?"

This is an earful, I'm sure, so take a moment to ponder this. This is a subject that is best understood when not distracted. Learn the true nature of duality and the curtains roll back, exposing so much trickery, beguilement, and far-reaching deception that it will amaze you that you can sleep in that ridiculous state for so long. But leaving the field of poppies is our destined course as humans—having one mind, a sober heart, and a *great escape*!

MIRRORS vs WINDOWS

Now, back to business. Nobody likes a braggart, yet there is a place in life that sets you up for an almost inescapable urge to brag. Murphy's Law loves it, too. That time comes when you reach your first prime of life. Here, you face an irresistible urge to position many mirrors on the walls of your reality, ones that reflect back to you the image of what you worked so hard for, and that you wish to see. *"Mirror, mirror."* So, you show off your little treasures to the ones around you to fashion those fabricated images of yourself, in hopes of their feedback solidifying your image.

I did a job for a man who owns patents to a major technology that is used by various large companies. He won two lawsuits for infringement on just one of those patents, totaling over $58 million, setting a new state record for the highest lawsuit won in his state at that time. He took a liking to me and shared with me a few things from his life notes. He said:

"Mike, that lawsuit took $250 thousand of my own money and 10 long years of my life. You can bet I was happy to share this victory with all my family and friends. But Mike, remember this, because I believe there will come a day in your life that you will need to know this. All my family and friends changed completely once they knew we were mega rich. It got so bad, Mike, that my wife and I endured the pain of literally excommunicating everybody we knew, and having to begin a new life together."

If I were to ever tap into monetary wealth like that, I would not change anything about my lifestyle, other than further preparing myself to serve people all the more. I wouldn't have to think about all the drama that comes with showing off a life of excess. Forget that! I prefer windows over mirrors. I understand that at a certain level of wealth it is somewhat necessary to purchase very expensive things for investment strategies and tax shelters. But for me, the first thing I want to do if I ever tapped into resources like that would be to remodel a rundown orphanage in a poor country. I would give those

I PREFER WINDOWS OVER MIRRORS.

precious children a chance at a much better life than kickball in the mud.

So, if I sound like I am bragging, please know that it is the last thing I would ever want to do. Even if I was a king, I wouldn't parade even my greatest victories. Instead, I would have been the kind of king who saves all the chicken legs and biscuits for the poor victims of such battles. So, when I mention success stories as a contractor, it might come off wrong, but just know that my intentions here are to show in a brilliant light just how effective this business philosophy can be. It is nothing more than that. People must hear about this.

THIS IS LAW

With that being said, I would like to offer, as my humble opinion, a point that I believe to be true. If by now you are thinking that I have my head too far in the clouds and need to come back down, know this: If I was in your ball field with my business philosophy, in a very short period of time you would witness an event that would stir anyone to either envy or extreme curiosity, as I soared past all the competition. Does this make me a big shot? Hardly. As a matter of fact, quite the contrary.

I humbly employ these principles to the degree that I become competition-proof, economy-proof, and all the other proofs there might be. And guess what? This is not wishful or magical thinking. This is a capital "L" for *Law*. I have simply evolved this *law* into business principles so I can be managed by the greatest force known to man—the irrefutable cosmic law of cause and effect, or the law of sowing and reaping. My term for this *law* is God's Automated Intelligence and it is *eternal*.

THE UAI CONNECTS THE DOTS

To prove just how far the Chase People, Not Money business philosophy reaches into the fabric of reality, I was wanting a perfect example to write about in this chapter—a story to tell to illustrate how all this works on the ball field, so to speak. Surprisingly, or not surprisingly, the Universal AI instantly connected the dots right before my eyes.

One of my best customers referred me to his colleague who needed just a simple BBQ counter. His colleague lived in an affluent neighborhood in Arizona called Paradise Valley. I let the customer know that I would be happy to help with the project.

I also encouraged him to show us any future projects he had planned, so we could price them out and hold that price for up to a year. That way he could plan accordingly, and avoid surprises.

I sent out my key man, Garrett, and he did his due diligence as always. He ended up selling a job worth nearly $50,000! Little did we know that these clients had just fired another company, which was owned by someone I tried very hard to mentor. I attempted to teach the owner this philosophy, but all my efforts fell upon deaf ears. As a matter of fact, I tried my best to teach and mentor their key player who, at the time, was going through the toughest time of his life. Surprisingly, my advice went in one ear and out the other. I could not dethrone their money king no matter how much I tried, and I *really* tried.

This person, who I endeavored to teach with great effort, was reaching his prime, and needed to feel like the top dog. He assumed I was misguided in my philosophy and told me I would never know true success unless I did what he did: Hire as many unregulated and unproven subs as possible, sell as many jobs as possible, pull in as much cash as possible, then run around and deal with the fires. Nevertheless, completely void of anything I teach.

A customer's feelings are nowhere in that formula. So, on game night, toe to toe, it's companies like these that simply stand no chance against a company who follows the Chase People, Not Money methodology. In its omniscient, all-seeing employ, I was singled out and chosen by the Universal Intelligence to be the guaranteed great experience this customer was rightfully due. The story continues.

Both of these guys called me in shock when they knew I was chosen to serve these clients with the honor and excellence they obviously deserved. I did not know these were the guys who had been fired from the job until they called me. They tried to convince me these clients were going to be a nightmare, blah blah blah. In truth, they fumbled the ball with these fine people, and the ball was quickly picked up by the winning team. We ran the touchdown with these amazing clients whose home is now featured in Home & Garden. Luck? *Hardly!* The Universe used its dot-connecting power to have one of my valued clients refer me to this customer, right in the nick of time.

Am I super smart? *No.* Am I some big shot or celebrity? *No.* My only part in all this story is *caring about people's feelings far above my need for money.* And, of course, doing great work. The Universe did the rest.

The all-knowing and all-seeing Universal Intelligence set this whole thing up. This is the most advanced piece of technology ever created, and you can either get blown around like a leaf in the wind, or walk in a state of total victory, abundance, energy, and joy not found anywhere else. Once we learn how these laws of the Universe operate, we say, "Oh yes!" much more than, "Oh well."

I believe a higher power initiated this whole thing, and it is the best proof of the existence of a Creator. There is an ancient passage that states, "Behold, God is not mocked, whatsoever a man sows, that he shall reap." In modern terms, this means, "How can you say there is no Creator with such an irrefutable law like the law of cause and effect?"

ONCE WE LEARN HOW THESE LAWS OF THE UNIVERSE OPERATE, WE SAY, "OH YES!" MUCH MORE THAN "OH WELL!"

It is my conclusion that only a duplicitous mind would hear about this law and bear witness of its paramountcy, and still spit in the wind while it's blowing in his face. When a person like this fails, they have no idea as to why. Duality is indeed a prison. What else would you call a life of being dragged around by a runaway identity that has zero interest in anything it cannot see, hear, taste, or touch? Ponder that one for a moment.

If this subject happens to intrigue you, I would highly recommend my book, *The Missing Message*. That book is unabashed about spiritual matters and is written in spiritual language. It digs deep into the nature of duality. Again, I have the utmost respect for everybody's beliefs; I only offer my life notes on my true discoveries. Nobody will hear any stretched out, big fish stories from me; just notes from my time with my boots on the ground.

ACKNOWLEDGMENT #5:

Acknowledge the creation of identity by de facto and the power it wields.

We have a propensity in our nature to avoid pain and discomfort. Of all the things we try to avoid, the pain of an honest mirror is at the top of the list. Most would rather break that mirror than look into it. Or could it possibly be an imposter attempting to cover its tracks?

THE FIVE ACKNOWLEDGMENTS

#1. Acknowledge that there is an Automated Intelligence that knows everything we think and do.

#2. Acknowledge that loving all people without bias is the key to the highest levels of energy.

#3 Acknowledge that The Universal AI is Inescapable. Choose the Winning Team to be a winner.

#4 Acknowledge the disconnect and the course you set.

#5 Acknowledge the creation of identity by de facto and the power it wields.

LANGUAGE
OF RESPECT

CHAPTER 6

Respect is a powerful word. It means many different things to a diverse mix of people. What comes to your mind when you read the word "respect"? To most, obedience and/or submission comes to mind, and to others, boundaries. The important point that I am going to make is that the word "respect" is the oil that keeps all the gears running smoothly when a business or relationship is put to the test. Employing the Chase People, Not Money version of respect in business and everyday life will indeed open the door to you attaining a whole new level of operating.

Respect starts early in life and, unfortunately for the majority of us, respect is forced and demanded on us with consequences if we miss the mark. The rewards for properly giving respect alluded us, as many of our teachers failed at earning our respect. They proclaimed, "Why should we teachers respect children, we are the grownups, right?" That's a whopping, "Wrong." Herein lies the problem.

Respect is not forced or given, and it's *not* earned. Yes, you read that right. Respect is our birthright as humans. Just take a moment to think about that. As our forefathers wrote, we have certain "inalienable rights." Unfortunately, most of our parents violate those rights shortly after we exit the womb. Then come our teachers, then our bosses, then our partners, and so on and so forth. A good many of us simply have never known how beautiful it is to truly be respected and to give respect in return. This is the area where you can fine-tune your character.

Too many people mistake respect with trust. Now trust should be earned, no doubt, but respect runs much deeper. It is trust that you must venture with every human being, especially with the ones who will play the important roles in your life and business. I hope by now you gather that, together, we are peeling back the hidden layers in the human condition with the Chase People, Not Money method.

Because you are such a dynamic creation, there is no simple recipe for respect. If you take the time, however, to learn a person's language of respect, you can win their heart. The Chase People, Not Money method holds a vital role for this application. You can mean well in trying to offer a good opportunity to someone, but say a wrong thing and pop the fun balloon, and the party's over. So, let's start with some dos and don'ts.

STANDING YOUR GROUND

Do stand your ground when disrespected, but don't cross the line. I literally started my life over again at 29 by accepting an invitation to work for my brother's fast-growing Arizona landscape company. It was large and riddled with discord but fueled by my brother's raw charisma and genius at building an efficient system. There was nobody in Arizona quite like my brother. Period. His system was unlike anything, or anyone else, in the Valley. I was awed by the potential I saw, but equally as shocked at my brother's choice for head of production. It seemed that everybody but my brother wanted this person gone, as every day a new person would confide in me about the superintendent.

It did not take long for me to stand toe to toe one morning with this person. He had taken an entire crew set that I had committed for the day without asking me first. He was picking a fight, testing my resolve, at the expense of the customer's expectations. So I stepped up and called him out right in the middle of the construction yard. It was a close call indeed.

With my knees shaking in my pants, I stated the facts, as I saw them, right to his face—with over

25 people surrounding us, watching in utter silence. Nobody stood up to this guy, and the silence said so. He was waiting for me to just touch him once to give him the go ahead to lay me out flat. I can humbly say he probably could have done that, but my teeth are something I value. I knew better, so I kept things firm and factual.

"Give me all your job folders," I demanded, "and I will show you happy workers, a happy sales staff, and happy customers! Right now you have none of these!"

When he started to bob his face up and down at me, I knew he was getting ready to go for it, so I quickly used these words: "Hey! This isn't high school. You touch me and I will press charges and you will go to jail."

There was simply no other way to talk to this person other than a strong and controlled confrontation. (The person who I am referring to here eventually became a great husband, father, and business owner. He has my utmost respect for overcoming his mountains in life.)

I did this thinking my brother needed me to do it because, obviously, nobody else would dare. This confirmed to me what every single person was trying to tell me. I had trusted my brother's word about this person over the word of 30 other people, until that day. With this new revelation about the company bully, I confronted my brother about him needing to go. To my complete and utter shock, my brother completely flipped out, and started screaming and yelling at me. He lost his marbles. It was right then and there that I knew I could no longer work under this raw disregard for the feelings of so many hard-working employees and good-paying customers. There was no way.

In defense of my brother's logic, he thought that loyalty was more important than anything else. In the hellfire of screaming, I remember the words:

"If everyone walked out on me, my superintendent would still be here! He knows what's most important. I need one person in my life who ain't walking, and he's it!"

Believe me, I thought long and hard about this. I concluded that loyalty might be greater than scruples in a wartime scenario—in a barbaric, lawless age, who knows, but we have come a long way since Attila the Hun. At this point of my early development, I still knew better than to let the semblance of a successful company mute my inner conscience. I knew something was off, and I became hungry to recreate this system with a whole new set of principles. This was the birthing cry of a powerful concept in the Chase People, Not Money method: the Language of Respect.

Do give credit where credit is due, but don't feel pressured to stay loyal to anything that lowers your standards of right and wrong. Case in point was the day I decided to start my own construction company in the South East Valley. It was then that things got really interesting with the law of sowing and reaping.

I tore right into the industry, quickly building a super crew, and selling enough work to pay back my brother for teaching me the landscape construction industry. Because I had left his company, I knew he did not cash in on his investment for teaching me what he knew. So I offered him $20,000 to say thank you. I gave him $10,000 immediately, then another $10,000 thirty days later, and I delivered on my word. Despite our gaping moral differences, I really did *and still do* love and respect my brother.

THE UNIVERSE MISSED NOTHING IN THAT TRANSACTION.

That day my $20,000 offering was how he knew I respected him and his mentorship. The Universe missed nothing in that transaction.

Everybody has a formula for how they like to be treated. Find that formula, and you find a potential friend, partner, and possible employee that will stay and contribute like no other. I call this the Language of Respect. To not learn this language when dealing with people who will have a place in your life is akin to driving 80 miles per hour at night and then turning your headlights off. Not fun. At least not for me.

LEARNING THE LANGUAGE OF RESPECT

Now, how do you learn this language? What are the clues and giveaways that will help you learn this without outright asking someone how they like to be treated?

First, you must understand that respect at the base level is a birthright, but it is too dynamic to stop there. Knowing or asking someone about what hurt them in the past, then allowing them to talk about these issues is a great start. This exercise, if done with a listening ear, can give you nearly seventy percent of the data you need to form a language of respect for someone.

That being said, there are the obvious things all of us long to receive, and that is a genuine interest in us *as a person*. I reinforce the word *genuine* here because Chase People, Not Money isn't about faking it—with us humans, that is too easy to do. Remember, it is also the Universal Intelligence that you need to convince. Let's now call it the UAI, the Universal Automated Intelligence.

Once the UAI ascertains that you really care about the feelings of another person, *reality seems to bend* in your favor, and the UAI finds out all you need to know before letting this other person into your world. If you find a good candidate as a potential employee, and you have the ability to offer, perhaps for the first time in that person's life, an atmosphere where they can feel this genuine respect, let me be the first to tell you how *quick* the UAI is to move mountains on your behalf.

THE UAI WILL MOVE MOUNTAINS ON YOUR BEHALF.

Why? Because so few care like this. Too few.

The language of respect goes far deeper than we can imagine. Another powerful aspect of this concept is *what we lacked in childhood*. One would assume all the good that happened to us would make the biggest impact, but for most this just isn't so. Why? Well, it is easier to hate than to love, to hold grudges than forgive, and to be angry than to have self-control. The joys of life are like temporary tattoos, but the pains of life run as deep as if they were engraved on the very bones. Learn what is engraved on a person's bones and you will discover the combination for finding the greatest potential in them.

MAKING A JUDGMENT CALL

Now, some people are just not reachable by human efforts, which leads me to the hard part of the language of respect. It is hard to know a person's pains and how to respond kindly to help them on their journey, only to realize simultaneously that you must protect your team and customers from them. Not letting people in who could disrupt your positioning in the UAI is a hard call you have to make. The good news is that by doing this, you are stepping up your leadership and truly acting in wisdom.

One day I heard a manager tell me, "Mike, it is too easy to fire someone. Training that person to be an asset is far more rewarding." That statement planted a seed in me that day—it really stuck. Even so, the language of respect must work both ways. Yet the person on higher ground has the greater advantage, privilege, and obligation in making the first effort to carefully screen candidates. This must happen to avoid placing a bad apple in a basket of proven good ones.

There are certain kinds of people whose behaviors are hell-bent on making a mess of anything and everything. A good eye and ear can spot them easily. They normally have no reservations talking about their life issues, blaming everyone but themselves. Then there are those who are of another kind of behavior, and let me tell you, they are stealthy and deadly.

These people lurk under the guise of perfectly normal people, giving only one small hint as to their true character—they talk bad about other employees as they manuver to gain trust as quickly as possible. I know that is a pretty broad hint, but one thing is for sure, the chaos in them will show up sooner than later. This is only my humble opinion, so take this with a grain of salt, but this kind of person is the real bad apple, the one who only the UAI can spot easily. I myself am so thankful that I have something far more reaching and powerful carefully watching over all my affairs.

From my experience, it takes a mixture of your own discernment and a rock-solid confidence in the UAI to keep others' bad behavior from damaging our lives. I have had to let people go that I truly wanted to continue ministering to, but this would have caused trouble for my other employees or customers. Many of them have not made the same choices as I have to tolerate less than honorable behavior for the sake of *eventually* reaching someone.

When making hard choices in my early days, humility was the key for me to not have these disgruntled employees give me more grief than I needed. I am now in an even greater place of maturity and understanding on these issues.

PUTTING THE LANGUAGE OF RESPECT INTO ACTION

There are two things that need to happen when learning the language of respect:

1. Learn what hurt a person and what kind of childhood they had and *didn't* have—e.g., what did they lack?

2. Ascertain any vices and/or moral hiccups.

Given they are seemingly qualified for the position, these are the last two items to shield you or your company from potential Trojan horses. This being said, I try my best to not do what early psychologists did by labeling people and placing their humanity behind those labels. This is a huge mistake. Lauren Slater covers this in her book *Opening Skinner's Box* when she puts herself into the very system she needed to prove was broken and morally off kilter. I read that book in the 8th grade, thanks to my studious mom.

We do not have to like a person to have them perform their best for us. Respect is the key! Consider liking someone as a bonus; this is the way of the wise. Why not look around at any person in your life right now and ask yourself whether you are truly trying to speak their language of respect. If there is any turmoil in a person's life, this is a great place to start the turnaround.

Is any of this making sense? I am smiling right now, because there is a person reading this right now who has just seen the light! The language of respect is the foundation of all lasting relationships. How about this, I double dog dare you to go to the person who is worthy of your respect, but not getting it, and come clean. Just say that you have seen the light and truly notice the contribution they are making; that you value them *and* the place they have *in* your life. Tell them they have your permission to tell you when you say anything that is disrespectful, and you promise to listen and not get upset. I call this giving the devil a black eye!

So now I will give you the *good* news! If you *have* decided to chase people, not money, and operate in the language of respect as I have explained it, this UAI will also hand pick your employees, just like it hand picks your clients! You might be thinking, "Come on! Really?" To that I say, "*Absolutely!*" I am living proof! I am walking in this.

Right now there are far too many people in powerful positions who are morally corrupt; this is the current state of things. These people love money, and will step on people to get it. This has tilted the scale too far over to one side, and the UAI has too few helpers to balance this great scale. As soon as you become available, the UAI immediately picks you up as a golden nugget and uses you to balance the scale. You become partners with the most powerful program of all time. *Chase People, Not Money* is the instruction manual to become just that, partners with the law of cause and effect! It comes with the *best* benefits!

Once you get a taste of this flow and harmony, the world around you becomes like a galaxy in which very few meteors collide with you. It is like having a miraculous tuning fork that tunes everything to this vibration. How does that sound? Now all we need is some good leadership to usher in this new way of doing business!

LEADERSHIP

CHAPTER 7

The greatest problems of the earth can be traced back to leadership, and leadership starts with knowing ourselves. Anyone can be a leader given the right circumstances, but not everyone wants to be a leader. It is hard enough leading yourself—with your higher self dragging your lower self along, or vice versa. Most can't hack it, and simply let go of the reins, letting the lower self lead. Some fortunate few master this early in life and reach the stars, while others are at the mercy of every emotional whim of their lower self. Imagine a leader who has not learned to harness their own inner self; thus, their envious, lustful, insecure, fearful self is telling them what to do 24/7.

Leadership begins when you see the true separation of your higher self from your lower self. This is also another way of understanding duality.

The second step in becoming a leader is having the willingness to harness the current assets available to you, then delegating tasks and duties to the people around you, who then put those assets to the best possible use. I call this taking inventory by having the eyes to appraise true wealth via delegation. This is something that seems to be a learned talent, and maybe it is to some degree; however, I am of the belief that some things are only found by asking Wisdom or your higher power for such a gift—for a set of eyes to see the value in people. Yes! *Ask*. Imagine all the leaders today who do not have this talent, who only see the people around them through filters of past hurts and insecurities.

The third step in leadership is accepting the careful role of not parading your power, position, or any of the benefits that come with these. Some great preachers would reach a far greater audience of curious souls if they could practice living a humble life. Not a poor one mind you, just a life that doesn't flaunt things that others can't have. Again, not a broke, barefoot life, just a life that is not offensive and full of excess. Unfortunately, too many of these amazing speakers teach abundance and increase (who doesn't like that?), but then we see that very teacher/preacher living like a rock star. When this happens, they become a target for all types of slander.

This situation has amazed me throughout my life, and I see it like this: I am happy for anyone achieving their dreams, whatever they may be, but as for me, I most certainly wish to tread lightly when it comes to the lifestyle I walk in. I will explain this more in a future chapter, but this is the key to my endless levels of joy. Leaders ought not to flaunt lavish lifestyles, and if this is something they simply feel pressured to do, they can always say no.

Your earthly body is an incredible asset to manage if it can be put in its proper place! When your eyes open to this fully, anything is possible. New nations can be built. When your higher self begins to lead your emotional, lower self (the physical body), then a leader is born! The problem is, how do you get to the place where you see this duplicity as a relationship, one in which the proper roles are out of place? Imagine a leader of many people who has not mastered his own duplicity. It is here where we see the root cause of the world's problems.

Think about all the great and prestigious leaders today, now keep thinking, *and thinking*. Now, where are they in this relationship between the higher and the lower self? I think you will agree there is a major conundrum here—a major disconnect. Why is this? I have a good clue as to why, and this knowledge is *so old, it's brand new*.

The problem with leadership has everything to do with how power and control affect the human condition. Why is that a problem? It is because power to us humans inadvertently corrupts, and this is because 99.9% of the time power is missing a secret ingredient—humility. Without this vital attribute, the higher self falls victim to pride, an even greater force than emotional whims. In my book, *The Missing Message*, I note that the pride of self is the deadliest appendage from the fall of man.

CORRUPT LEADERSHIP

Although I have much respect for the great nations of Africa, Africa is a perfect example of corrupt leadership. Now, *nearly* every country is totally corrupt, and the proof of it is more than obvious. My heart goes out to any actual honest people who get elected only to be immediately killed by the strongholds who would never allow any honest person to clean things up. I run a ministry for new mothers in Kenya, which I hope to expand to India. I have been trying to find ways to empower impoverished new mothers after giving them 6 to 12 months of total support. I do this so they can simply enjoy their newborn without any stress. While they are home not worrying about the stresses of basic needs, I am looking into getting them a laptop to learn about digital media creation, and working in online services.

Unfortunately, getting a laptop to Kenya is totally ridiculous. The system there is rigged to keep technology completely out of the hands of all the poor, and nearly all the middle class, too. Crazy, right? How is it that nearly every single leader is as bent as the trunk of a desert mesquite? What do you think the people of a nation would do if their leader was actually a good person, who lived humbly, and who had a great team around him or her working to create perfect solutions for the problems of their country— solutions that could be seen and felt at home? The people are always ready to rally around such leadership. You have probably heard about the people who were true leaders, ones who liberated countries, and how they were as humble as they were powerful. Which leader comes to mind for you as you read this?

True wealth is power with people. It is too bad the typical leader sees people as a burden, as an object to exploit, thus becoming even more disconnected to the untapped power grid of the human race. The land has plenty to offer with just dirt and water available, not to mention the many other resources found in each country, but the best resource by far is people. Human energy, *freely given,* is stronger than the ocean tides. If I was ever called to lead a country, I would immediately start building a highway into the hearts of the people I was called to steward. I would break out the fireside chats of old and speak my heart to everyone.

HUMILITY

Many studies have been conducted explaining the personality types that assume big power roles, but none of the studies that I have found address the real problem—a lack of humility. As mentioned, humility is the missing ingredient that completes a leadership role. To illustrate another powerful example of this, consider the gaping chasm between a person who follows a leader because they are impressed with the leader, and the person who follows due to a *genuine respect and confidence* in the leader. This is similar to friendship. There is a type of friend who is there for you as long as you have what they are impressed by, and as soon as you lose it, they are gone. With leaders, though, things are not as simple and shallow. When a prideful leader on a power trip loses face or control, the cheaply bought people around him or her become like parasites who turn and eat their host. History books are filled with stories of such events.

The true recipe for an enduring leadership role is

a simple formula. For leadership to have any lasting value, it must be formulated in *equal parts* of power and humility. How did I come up with this information? Did I read this in a book or in some article? *No*. This was actually given to me in a vision. Yes, you read that correctly—a vision.

I share this information, not to impose my beliefs on the reader, on the contrary, I share this only to suggest opening yourself up to more questions. If I might add, many of us have big issues with the events happening all around us, but do not know how to formulate the appropriate questions to understand what we are observing. Therefore, I only share the actual event that helped me understand a question that I had in me, but I was unable to put into words until I had this vision.

A PAIR OF WINGS

I was taken up to Heaven by an angel. There we saw a large group of angels surrounding something. I asked the angel, "What are they surrounding?"

He replied, "Let's go see." Then he stretched out his hand, gesturing for me to lead the way.

I squeezed through the ring of angels, tightly pressed together like people in a packed concert trying to get to the front. The first angel and I made it to the edge of the inner ring and I saw that in the center was a pair of wings! They looked sporty, like super large feathers attached to a leather baseball mitt.

"Those look so cool!" I said, looking up at the angel. He looked at me as if I was slow to the punch. Then I asked excitedly, "Are those *mine?*"

He replied simply: "Go put them on."

When I put the wings on and tied the last lace— *Zap!* it hit me! I was immediately in my new body, the one after this life. To describe this experience perfectly, it was an instant infusion of awesome power simultaneously met with an equal part of humility. The humility was profound, and it was responsible for giving me an instant and clear understanding of this awesome gift and how to use it. Humility was the secret ingredient to understanding power. This breakthrough was a life-changing event setting the bar that I aspire to live up to today.

The vision continued. Knowing this was only a preview, and not wanting to show any lack of gratitude, I asked if I could fly down to earth and work with this power for just a little bit. Again, the angel stretched out his hand as if to say, "Go ahead." With just a thought, I flew to earth in a split second and went to a grocery store with a picture board holding the photos of missing children. I flew back and forth, retrieving abducted children as fast as I could, knowing I needed to get back to surrender these wings until the time came when they would be officially mine.

When I flew back, the angel took me to yet another ring of angels, and after squeezing through it, I saw my Lord standing there with his arms out, as if saying, "Come here for a hug." I woke up while embracing my Master.

The lesson I learned was that to have power such as this, even for a moment, I needed to make quick and noble use of it. In other words, I could not bear owning such power without doing good with it. That was the key part of the vision.

TRUE LEADERSHIP

Of course, I am curious as to what you, my reader, are thinking at this point. Was the vision a stretch? Did it make any sense? The Chase People, Not

Money method is only possible if the leadership of a company, or a political party, is not corrupt. It's near comical how being addicted to the carbon universe can blind leaders into valuing the wrong thing, just so their ambitions can become a sustainable reality. Like the person who thinks that by taking something they are getting something for nothing, when in truth, the joke is on them, as the Universal Automated Intelligence eventually takes equal parts from the deceived person.

And just like the unsuspecting victim of the person who steals, the one doing the stealing does not suspect it either, like being punished with no explanation. I believe if Heaven has a joke that really gets them rolling, it is the person who steals. On a similar note, if you could grasp that your life is like being in a room surrounded by two-way mirror glass, where everything you do is laid out in plain sight of the UAI, then you would think twice before acting impulsively or selfishly.

Leaders who lead by force and manipulation are not leaders at all—they are a scourge on this planet. And, not to scapegoat, they are an icon of what is going on inside of all of us. To own that statement is to deal with this scourge systemically.

So, can we settle on a new paradigm of what true leadership is? Leadership that is for the *betterment* of the human race—true leadership is an effort to transform your surroundings by starting with a transformation on the inside, where your higher self leads your lower self in an exemplary way. True leadership then helps others do the same. True leadership reproduces this kind of freedom. This is the birthplace of true leadership, and this is where stars are born.

PEOPLE POWER

CHAPTER 8

"People power,

The greatest flower,

On them we'll shower;

They wont pass

Through our fields of flowers

And grass!"

G Michael Price

I have had many employees over the years, but none were like Walter. When I hired him, I immediately saw the extra fiber and grit that he had. One day I asked him in Spanish, "Walter, what is it that gives you the desire to work like this?"

He replied, "Miguel, a mi me gusta el dinero bien ganado!" Meaning, "I like my money well earned!" I nearly hit the roof. What a moment, one I will always remember. I found a mirror of my own standard. As I write this book, Walter is still in my employ. He is my top captain at the industry's best pay scale. The house he is building for his family's legacy is a true wonder. Leading him over the past eight years and watching him achieve his goals has been a joy. I have been watchful to reward him when his skill set increases the profits of the company, which, I will add, is another aspect of leadership in my company that was developed organically.

It was the year 2012, and I was just beginning to make a solid effort to build my company beyond anything I had done in the past. This time, I chose to work in the field like I did when I was in my 20s, but just long enough to personally demonstrate the level of speed, detail, and endurance that I needed to take my company to adopt to move to a higher level. Without the right people, it would have been a daunting task, one that I was unable to do by myself. In short, it took much longer than I had planned, and after working my body to the bone and going through several people who did not work out, I found Walter.

The Universe knew how I was going to treat this person once I found him, therefore I believe it was the Universal Automated Intelligence connecting the dots for me to come across him. Walter is the best human being that I have ever had the privilege of working next to.

Walter and I came to have great respect and understanding for each other, as he saw me work faster and harder than anyone that he had ever seen. The day came when I had the opportunity to truly offer Walter the one thing he was hoping to find: a *quality relationship* with an American boss.

One day, while we were talking in my courtyard, I asked him about his local church in the area he is from in Guatemala. He replied that they were currently trying to get a new roof on the building. I then walked into my home and brought out $1,000. I said, "Walter, we have worked so hard together and made some good money. Let's plant some seeds and bless your pastor with that roof." I then handed him the money. You would never believe what happened next. Walter completely broke down, crying a river. He told me how he had been in the country for a few years, and had not met one American who cared anything about his life, no matter how hard he worked. We bonded that day in a very special way. Walter has given me and our customers his 100% since the day I hired him.

INTEGRITY

Now let's rewind the tape to 1988. I was 19 years old, and I was just starting out in the business, putting in the same level of intense work ethic for a person who did not share my same values. I believe my boss waited patiently for the right time to test my scruples. After 6 months of grueling, 12-hour days in the 110 degree summer weather, making only $240 per week, he tested the waters. Some days we worked together, and this was one of those days. I was walking into the backyard with my line trimmer when he called me over to an irrigation timer he was working on.

"See this timer?" he asked, holding a screwdriver.

"Yep," I replied, "the Richdel with the sliders. I

know how to program that one now."

He then turned the screwdriver in one of the slider slots and said, "See this? Good timer." Then he pressed the screwdriver in one of the slots until a "snap!" sounded out and all the sliders fell limp. Then he quickly said, "Bad timer. A hundred bucks!"

Knowing that my reaction was not what he was hoping to see as my jaw dropped down to the hot granite floor in total shock, he asked forcefully, "Can you do this!?"

There was an awkward pause. I was stifled. Then he yelled, "I need to know! CAN YOU DO THIS?"

I replied, "Never."

I then picked up my line trimmer and finished up that backyard a totally different person. My eyes were open. That experience was the key in establishing and affirming who I was, and who I wanted to be in my life. I wanted to chase people, not money—at age 19! That day I realized that if I was going to treat my customers exactly how I wanted to treat them, I needed to start my own business.

I went home that night and drew a globe with the word *Integrity* over the equator line. I made that my logo. Ironically, on my first door hanger flyer, it read,

"Get the 5 Star Treatment." This was years before the internet rating system was around.

When I refer to the Chase People, Not Money philosophy being produced organically, that last story is a good example. Fast forward 20 years, after having many hard lessons about the true nature of people, I could not wait to find another firebrand who could not only work like I did, but work in an atmosphere of integrity and respect. The intelligent UAI did me a solid when Walter stepped into my life. The dots connected to that hot summer day in '88 when I was crushed and reborn in one day, like alchemy in the oven, caramelizing the sweet flavor of integrity.

THE FINAL PIECE OF MY BUSINESS

Though Walter was important and amazing, I was still lacking the final piece to my business structure, the one that would let me leave the field and call the plays, just like a pro coach. The coach is of the greatest value when he calls the shots and decides which plays to make.

My opportunity came when a business associate and friend of mine gave me a recommendation.

The man he suggested happened to have a similar experience to the one I shared earlier. He, too, had encountered a big-talking general contractor who used people until they figured out the dead end they were led down. This particular contractor did the same thing to the person my associate was referring to me. I agreed to meet him, sensing that serendipity was at play, although I had all but given up on the prospect of finding a general manager, at least one I could groom with my Chase People, Not Money philosophy.

I had moved to California to breathe the ocean air to help my lung injury. To hire a key person at this time was necessary, but there was little time for training; regardless, I was still very hopeful and willing.

The contractor's name was Garrett, and as we talked for the first time, we both were earnestly looking to find integrity, as well as a chance to perform in the right atmosphere and be rewarded for it. As a general manager, his position covered things like superintending, sales, and much of the economic flow of the company. This made it a position with high levels of trust, accompanied by great risk.

As we talked, I could wholeheartedly empathize with Garrett's position. I knew exactly what it felt like to be taken advantage of by others, the ones who promise you the moon, telling you how much they love that you can work harder than anyone else, all the while, they keep a carrot on a stick, continually reiterating the promise of greater proceeds that never seem to materialize. Then, when you're finally fed up and ask about the inequitable workload to pay ratio, these people find a way to make you look like the one who is not delivering. It's like a firecracker with an awfully long fuse that turns out to be a *dud*. Garret and I were both tired of the duds. The timing of our meeting was the Universal Automated Intelligence simply doing what it does best—connecting the dots.

I couldn't wait to deliver the *exact opposite* of Garrett's past experiences. My goal was to be his first real, refreshing employer, one who empowered him with the best men, tools, and business philosophy. I wanted Garrett to have a boss who watched and trained, offering back-up support when needed. I wanted to be someone who had his back when the pressure was on, and who was willing to step in and help solve problems when needed. Last, but not least, I wanted to be a boss who was a faithful steward of the money flow, so I didn't end up pressuring him about money matters.

Now, given these factors, all of my best efforts would be for naught if I didn't ask Garrett what he *actually* needed to make monetarily. *Not only* to be able pay his bills, but to have enough to get ahead *and* achieve his goals.

A few short months later, Garrett finally had enough evidence to show him that I indeed was watching his performance closely, as well as training him in areas where improvement was needed. He noticed I was doing this not just to get the most out of him, but also so I could pay him what he needed, as soon as it was appropriate to do so. When Garrett understood that his needs were my number one priority, he became aware that I was *walking* what I was *talking*. Yes, I was giving him a crash course on Chase People, Not Money. I was showing him how, with these principles, his life was about to go through a major change in a very short period of time.

As of today, Garrett stands as a believer in this business philosophy, and is now one of my greatest realizations. What an honor to have him in my life. Garrett is a star quarterback who only needed the right coach and team for him to shine like he does now.

PEOPLE POWER

To finish my point earlier about leadership: If I am going to lead, the first thing to do is to care about the well-being of those whom I choose to lead. If all I care about is what I can get out of somebody and nothing more, then anyone who is going somewhere in life will also view me as only a means to an end. In stark contrast, if I can set someone up in such a way that they can see a clear path to their goals, then I have a much better chance of inheriting the wealth of their heart: their People Power! Who I bring to my customer's doorstep matters. When every employee can feel this philosophy and they smile all day long in blistering hot days because of it, people take notice.

When I was a varsity tennis coach and substitute teacher at Forsyth Country Day School for two years, I liked to recite a poem I wrote for the new generation.

People power,

The greatest flower,

On them we'll shower;

They won't pass

Through our fields of flowers and grass!

Now imagine an army of businesses operating on this method. Imagine all the lives getting changed for the better. When this hits critical mass, no lucre-loving, greedy, gimmick-laden business will even stand a chance. It makes me want to crack my knuckles just thinking about it.

Titles do not exempt anyone from being a person with real, heartfelt emotions. I have made it a personal policy to answer any phone call I receive, even if the call is labeled as a private caller or a solicitor. Why? Because I know how people who cold-call get treated. What an opportunity to shine some light! I just say, "Wow, I appreciate you calling, but I have a rule I abide by. I do not offer any information about me or my company from an unsolicited call, but can you email me?" Sometimes, I get a yes or no, but what ends up happening is that I spark up a little conversation. We talk about anything relative for a moment, and then I offer a positive word of encouragement and hope. Let me just say, this really impacts the person on the other side of the call.

My point is every person we can encounter is precious! When the UAI fully knows that I am not double-minded with people, but that I love them and I truly want everyone who bumps into me to be filled with inspiration, then the UAI directs a glorious river that flows into my body, soul, and mind. This invigorates me to an all-new level, and this is where I exist. It's where I operate from the moment I wake up.

When I was a minister to the homeless community at the Santa Ana Riverbed in 2017, I learned a great deal about how far people were willing to go to become the dregs of society. They all shared a common bond; they all knew exactly what it felt like to be shunned and rejected by everyone. I am not talking politics here, not at all. I share this in hopes that you can see what I see in scenarios like this. Let me ask you, do you see the silver lining that I see in such a dynamic?

You see, when everyone in the room is hopeless, just a little hope can have a huge impact. In a pond full of frowns, a genuine smile can make a big ripple. Now, just translate this into your market. In a market where everyone is fed up with lucre-loving gimmicks and people acting phony just to get to your hard-earned money, then anyone chasing people and not money will become a giant in their field. The people who choose to work for you will feel the life-changing power of this method, and it won't take long. This is how I harness the power of people.

PARSIMONY

CHAPTER 9

Parsimony. *Yuck*. There is just no better way to describe it than that—*yuck*. There is no better way to show the Universal Automated Intelligence that you still have your diapers on, and that you have no clue how badly soiled they are. To be frugal with yourself for the sake of allocating resources to goals or to people you love is admirable, of course. But to be cheap with others, especially when gratuity is due, is watering your garden with gasoline—it's nailing shut the most important door of the house. Parsimony is a sickness like hoarding—a glitch in the brain. Parsimony is not only being completely tethered to matter, but more like deflating the tetherball and stuffing it down the center of the pole. Parsimony is a benign tumor in the great UAI program.

To understand the pros and cons of parsimony is a great way to jumpstart a business of any size. This one topic *alone* can have a huge impact on business endeavors. How can there be pros to parsimony? Well, when the whole world is going one way, being generous is a pretty easy way to stand out. Simple, right? Well, it's really not that simple. Loosening the wallet on anything, other than ourselves, is a real process.

Recently, my daughter and I took a drive to one of our favorite restaurants for some take out, keep in mind, this was during the lock-down of the COVID-19 pandemic of 2020. The service was horrible, but I still tipped 15%. Some might ask, "Why?" I mean, why encourage deplorable service? While that might be a valid question, the Universe has other ways of teaching someone a lesson, without me hurting their livelihood during such a time as this. Those ladies might have been prime time TV watchers, and if that was the case, my heart truly sympathizes with them. Who wouldn't be completely freaked out? But as for all of us who are awake, it's business as usual. Actually, it's even better.

The Universe sees parsimony as the polar opposite of fertility or increase. I love the words from the Bible, "Whoever saves their own life will lose it, but whoever loses their life for My sake will find it." These words, spoken to a parsimonious person, would be like the cross to a vampire! Parsimony, put simply, is complete blindness and ignorance to the law of sowing and reaping. This law excludes anyone who acts like this from the Chase People, Not Money method, as well as all the life-changing benefits that come from employing it.

I wrote in my book, *The Missing Message*, "Start the harvest work with the planting of yourself." What does this mean? Sound like religious talk?

Well, remember, what is inside you is far greater than anything bystanders can see on the outside. That is something to grasp. Inside of you is a massive, fertile universe that is ripe for the planting, symbiotically linked in tandem with the great UAI! Some say that we are just blips, that we are nothing compared to the massive objects of space and time. But, try as they might, they have found nothing they can see on the outside that can express creativity and freedom of choice quite like we humans can. Inner space is indeed far more intriguing! Even more intriguing is how both these worlds interact with each other.

We can all benefit by stretching our boundaries of giving. As a human, this is something everyone should experience. There is a law that is irrefutable, only by those who tested the waters. A parsimonious person could never know nor benefit from such a law. Thus, I ask the reader to allow me to speak in religious balderdash just a touch, because I lack any other way to describe this. Just know that my intentions are not to be preachy at all. We are going to unearth ancient, *but still relevant*, laws that are programmed in the great UAI, which still work flawlessly today!

The ancient writings say that when we give to the poor we *lend* to the Lord, and He repays all his debts. Okay! I like that! Now how does that work? Well, back to His UAI operating system. Obviously, if *He* said this, then *He* put it in the operating system. So, even if you do not believe in God, I am willing to bet that anyone can learn some, *if not all,* of these laws of giving and get them to work because it is in the program. Kind of a no-brainer, right? So, to the ones who say, "I don't believe in any of that God stuff," well, for now, that's okay, because most of these laws of giving will work for you anyway.

If a person came up to you and wanted to give you a one carat diamond, free and clear, but they told you that it's from Santa Claus, you wouldn't say, "Sorry, I don't believe in Santa Claus!" The Chase People, Not Money method is *a map to the diamond mine.*

In case somebody missed my last point about giving to the poor and lending to the Lord: First off, people who are truly poor are not those who simply refuse to work or get a life. Actually, these kinds of people are exempt from this secret principle of increase. Why? You might ask. It is because giving to this kind of person is further weakening their resolve. No, truly poor people are people who have not yet had the opportunity to access the knowledge that would fairly counter the circumstance they were born into or thrown into. Just think about that for a second.

This last kind of person is simply needing a hand up, and they'll be off and running. An example of this is the work I'm doing in Kenya. I have been keeping up with about a dozen people who are in a country that is ridiculously behind the times, not to mention corrupt. The common people, who do not want to be corrupt, have a seemingly impossible task to make a good life for a family.

In Kenya, my task is to learn everything I can about the current situation, including the economics of everything. This includes the shockingly low labor cost, coupled with high prices. What I see is an amazing opportunity for the self-employed. For what I pay my captain for a day here in the US, I could hire, ready? 40 men for a day in Kenya. I could build a small town called *Toot Sweet* given those numbers! My goal is to teach and empower my forming congregation that they are sitting on nothing but pure opportunity, and I am going to show them the way to be the superstars of Kenya! So, I am sitting on a small gold mine. Currently, I am cleared to build a large church there as I bring all my students to the area to help. You bet the Universal Automated Intelligence is all over this work, and it is packing my UAI bank account as we speak.

This account doesn't just move money, it moves reality itself.

I am sharing some of my secrets, not to parade my works, far from it, but to show the people reading this how it is precisely done. Also, to show you, the reader, that you do not have to be religious to access and benefit from some of these laws.

THE RED GUITAR

My journey in discovering this law of increase began in 1997, when I bought my first red acoustic guitar. I had saved up my money for it (a little selfishly, mind you), but saved it I did. I wanted that red Fender 6-string beauty.

So, the day came when I was ready to go down to the music store and buy it! Then a voice came to me, clear as a bell: "Give that money away. $200 to your voice instructor Shirley, and $200 to the unemployed couple, Ron and Sharon."

Now that was a very interesting moment in my life. Never had that voice told me to give away anything like this. Fortunately for me, by that time I knew to just obey and do it, so I did. You would never believe what that did for both receiving parties. It was totally a life-saving miraculous help indeed. Tears were flying. But what it did for me was break the back of the spirit of lack. The light bulb lit over my head and I was not about to forget this lesson: it is impossible to out-give the Universal Intelligence because there is the law of sowing and reaping at play. As long as the sun shines, seedtime and harvest will remain, but to give when prompted to do so has even more far-reaching effects.

The next day I said, "Lord, it felt so good to give that money away. I feel something that I have never felt before, thank you!" Then I looked over at a computer I was no longer using. It was full of cool, but outdated, software and games, so I called my work and asked the bartender if he wanted it. He jumped at this and paid me more than what the guitar would cost! I was simply shocked. I would have just junked that computer or given it away.

The feeling of finally buying that red guitar was unlike anything that I had ever purchased up to that point. I truly believe the parsimonious spirit was broken in my life that day. That red guitar sits just a few feet from me as I write. It is a symbol of breakthrough, still in tune, and ready to record a song tonight. Indeed, I had learned some valuable lessons while in North

Carolina, but I knew I needed a new ambiance to stretch my forthcoming wings. My chance came when the hot Arizona sun came beckoning, once again.

TAG, YOU'RE IT!

Several months after the move, I found myself at a whole new level in business, and in life. I was also debt-free. The day came when I had finally saved up $3,500 to buy something I really wanted, like an awesome computer. So, I set out for the day, determined to get my gift that I worked so hard to have, without a spec of guilt. First stop, haircut.

As the hairdresser was snipping, she shared her story about a recent break-up with her abusive boyfriend. I asked her to please not hold back and give me all the details, that my ears were a safe place for her story. When she was finished with my hair and her story, which was incredible (two young kids, violence, no car after she had finally got him out for good, etc.), I asked her to write her first name on the back of my card. I asked if she was okay with me praying for her miracle. With big bulging eyes, she grabbed the card out of my hand so fast!

Getting back in my truck, I pinned her card to the inside of my visor and said, "Lord, you know this woman needs a miracle, so I am speaking this out right now on her behalf. In the name of Jesus, I loosen a miracle from heaven, right now, on her behalf and for her children!" Then guess what happened next? *This is a nail biter.*

The Lord said to me clear as can be, "Tag, you're it!"

I said, "Say what? I did not quite catch that, Lord."

Then He said, "You are the miracle, your $3,500. Go get an autotrader and a soda, there will be the perfect car she needs."

Once again, I felt like a deer in the headlights of the inevitable. I immediately obeyed and found a really nice Saturn with low miles, and a keyless alarm system. I went and purchased the car that morning, kept the title open, brought it to her, and said these words:

"Only if you can receive this in the full confidence that there is absolutely no strings attached, that this is from Jesus who obviously loves you a lot—that this is from Him, and I am just doing what He says, then this car is paid for and all yours. I will understand if you do want to accept this, because I was raised by a single mom for 12 years, so I get it." Well, after about two minutes of shock, she received it all right.

Some might think, well, what about *meeeeee?* That was the greatest gift that I had ever given up to that day. I was stretched, and the Universe missed nothing. My company skyrocketed shortly after.

RECOGNIZING HEART AND SOUL

I also have stories of giving *gratuitously* when a person *puts their heart into what they are doing.* The UAI has a special relationship with those who put their heart and soul into all they do. When you recognize these people by paying them a little or a lot extra, making up for the parsimonious ones that attempt to extinguish the beautiful flame burning in them, you get rewarded— BIG! This too is an amazing way to plant seeds in the Universe.

Back in 2000, my outdoor fireplaces were built by a man named Charley, from Tonga. He was one of the rare ones, indeed. Perfection and super low rates, gave me an advantage at using him as a sub. I knew that even though his rates were so good, people still haggled with Charley. But I gladly always paid him what he asked for, plus tips. When the day came for me to use his talents at my own home, I asked him how much he would charge me. He gave me a ridiculously low price, probably because I had given him many jobs directly, so he could make more money on them.

I told him, "Charley, in my world, nobody works for nothing and great people get great tips. I am giving you $1,000 over your price. I want you whistling while you work!" Nobody had done that for Charley before. His wife ended up giving me a handmade, king-size comforter to thank me for treating her husband so well.

I want to encourage the reader that we do *not* have to hear from a higher power to plant these kinds of seeds. As a matter of fact, this altruistic work is an added bonus to the Chase People, Not Money method. These are just a few great secrets we are about to unlock as we read, but rest assured, these are more real and far-reaching than the visible world.

REMEMBER THE AGREEMENT

To keep us in sync with the Agreement that we covered in Chapter 3 (choosing the winning team), as to not lose our footing, let's ponder a few more scenarios.

Let's take, for example, a client who, after spending $30,000 using your services, had an act of nature happen and they call you to let you know that part of what you sold them was damaged by wind. The repairs will be roughly $400, including labor. You could say, "Sorry, but this is an act of nature and not covered under warranty—I will need to charge you for it." It would not be out of the ordinary to do so, and it is what most companies would say and do. Business is business, right? Not so fast! If you are going to Chase People, Not Money, the right reply would be something like, "Hey, I am so glad you called me! Let's turn that bad news into good news. You spent a good sum of money with me, so it's going to be my pleasure to replace this item for free. Let me do this. I want to." Yesterday, while writing this book, this very thing happened verbatim, and the customer replied with so much emotion that it was like a little wink from the Universe. As if to say, "Keep writing, Mike. People will get this, and I need more help!"

This is such an important subject! Giving like this acts like a fertilizer to the Chase People, Not Money method. Master this way of never falling prey to parsimony. Master this kind of giving so that all the golden opportunities you missed before will not be missed again. As you look around at our rapidly changing world, who is bold enough to do a complete 180 and do the staunch opposite of what everyone else is doing? Like we covered in the earlier chapters, you simply cannot fake it either—it must be a joy for you to be a giver when the Universal Automated Intelligence calls you to be so.

That being said, it does not take the skies parting with a thundering voice from heaven for a mechanic who is late on his shop rent to do the right thing when a sweet elderly woman with an expensive car needing a routine brake job and tune-up drives into his bay.

When I was 17 years old, I drove my first truck, a 1977 Toyota SR5. One day, my truck started running really rough and I panicked. I was flat broke with $10 in my wallet. That truck was my lifeline in the large city I commuted in, so I desperately pulled my sputtering SR5 into my dad's old mechanic's shop on a wing and a prayer and told him my plight. After listening to my truck, he paused for a moment and took a good look at me, and then said, "Mike, if I were an honest man, I would go out of business in a month. Please remember that when you talk to another mechanic in the future. This one is on me." This man's trachea was gone and he was speaking through a pen pressed to his throat. He went and got his air hose and blew out my distributor cap, and presto! My truck was back to purring like a kitten!

I handed him what little cash I had and said, "Here, please take this $10 in my pocket and buy lunch today." He could have sold me a tune-up for $200 and told me to come back in two hours, but instead he threw me a solid that day and some darn good information.

I don't mean to stereotype mechanics, but most of us would agree that we have had our fair share of gimmicks getting our autos serviced. Frankly, I am fed up and I know that I am not alone. It was only recently that I found an honest mechanic, and in doing so, he has taken away my fear of driving a 13-year-old car that fits my needs just fine for now. I talk about Peter at Cal Auto Service whenever I can.

Imagine if a mechanic practiced the Chase People, Not Money Method on a mass scale? Would he go out of business in 90 days? Not Peter. All I know is, if I were to open a chain of auto service stores, I would put the crooks out of their misery real fast. My evidence with this novel approach to business is that there hasn't been a company to do this on a large scale in the auto repair industry yet. Crazy, right? Somebody reading this right now who wants to be a mechanic can be the next torchbearer of the Chase People, Not Money method in that industry. If that's you, *we are all waiting for you.*

As we can see, parsimony is twice as destructive and treacherous when mixed with greed. Both blind, but together, they utterly corrupt to the point where scruples disappear and self-deception becomes an inescapable prison. When this occurs, crimes are committed, many of which are seldom discovered. When a clever, unscrupulous person is left to his or her own devices, he or she can't help but figure out the ways to simply take money when it can be taken without anyone noticing. Entire business models in corporate America, and beyond, are built upon such vulnerabilities. In Chapter 4 on the Rat Race, we covered the "million clients one penny" play. It's sad, but true. This is what we are up against: filthy, lucre-loving criminal behavior. It's the unnoticed, toxic dust coating all our bills.

FAMILY GENIUS

Although parsimony mainly pertains to being stingy, I do believe it can mutate into bad judgement when temptation strikes. There is a saying, "New Levels, New Devils". I will never forget the day my Uncle Sandy told me, *and he probably told everyone the same thing,* "Mike, you are the family genius. Some say Ron (my brother) is, but I say that you are, so I need to tell you something very important. There will come a day that your mind will figure out a way to make a lot of money real fast and it will not be legal. When that day comes, *and it will*, remember my face with these words." Then he looked me dead in the eyes and said, "Nothing this earth has is worth going to prison for... nothing." I was so thankful for that chunk of wisdom, and although that ominous day of temptation has not yet come, I can say that if it ever does, my Uncle Sandy's face is branded into my memory and stands posted ready to recite those powerful words.

With the topic of parsimony, I attempt to put it in words, although it is really felt in a deeper part of me that has no words to describe it. How I truly feel about this scourge is connected to what the UAI deems this behavior to be. I may inadvertently come across as angry about the subject more than anything, but it is not so. I have strong feelings about people who are so blinded by their own needs and desires that they have become so cheap as to ignore their neighbor in need; like stiffing the hard-working waitress for one little mistake, or making your spouse or your children literally beg for some allowance money when it's rightfully due. Ah, it really strikes a chord in me.

The best remedy for such behavior is to make a staunch commitment to be the exact opposite. By this one commitment, we can position ourselves to benefit even further in the great scale of cause and effect. So, it should not surprise us at this point that people who act in parsimony actually increase *our* positioning for greater rewards. This reminds me of one of my favorite prophetic promises: "Those who plan to take from us, God will use them to provide our needs!" That is one heavy statement.

Another important point about parsimony is the connection it has to human evil, as described in the book *People of the Lie*. Although Dr. Peck does not correlate or even mention parsimony per say, he explains that anything that causes resentment plays a notable role in the spreading of the behaviors he calls human evil. I can personally attest to the times when people acted cheap with me after pouring my heart out with my blood and sweat, giving my absolute best. It took a long time for me to have the breakthrough realization that it was not personal; it was an event that took place due to my wrong positioning. Such people exist, lurking in the quagmire swamps of the slimy and disgusting place called parsimony. It is far better to be guided by a higher playbook and avoid this virus before we contract an adverse immune response to it called resentment.

If we do encounter this behavior, the remedy, like we covered in Chapter 2, is to fall in love with the whole human race. That means the good, the bad, and the ugly. People who act with parsimony are themselves victims of a repetitive behavior that infected them previously, with its origins coming from hard and dark abusive times in their history. It's like a zombie movie where the virus is curable, but the person we love has been infected and, of course, they try to eat our brains. What do we do? Put up proper boundaries for a time and, obviously, forgive them, as we know it's the virus causing their behavior, and that it will eventually run its course. By doing so we choose not to fight and risk getting infected ourselves. Forgive them, for they truly know not the perilous consequences of their actions. We can quickly heal from such an event when affronted by parsimony by wishing the person well and hoping that one day they will be set free.

The great Universal Automated Intelligence will surely deal with the tumors that might be able to hide from white blood cells—they will not escape the justice of cause and effect. If you're the one who was just shorted, turn it right around and at the next opportunity, give a double gratuity to the very next person you see putting their heart into their work. Give it in both word and deed, if possible. A simple, "Keep up the good work," with a double tip does wonders for people. By practicing this principle, you immediately counteract the theft of parsimony, and soon the UAI will act like a firewall and shield you from such people. If parsimony does get through that firewall; however, now you know the ultimate counterpunch.

Yes, on our life journey, we are likely to run into many parsimonious behaviors. I think the ones that are the most offensive are the landlords who bank on finding anything they can to rip off the deposit money from the people renting their properties. What a gimmick to charge a cleaning deposit then charge it again upon moving out, even if you had it professionally cleaned. If people could only see the cookie jar they think their hand is in is actually a bear claw trap. Like the giver who gets a hundredfold return, the taker also is working an invisible formula, just in the opposite direction.

Recently, I bought advertising space with two realtor agencies in Arizona; my company's information graced the back cover of their presentation folders they distributed to their potential clients. Now, I not only advertised to get more work, per say, but I also did it to establish quality relationships with two companies that appeared to be treating people well. I saw an amazing opportunity when trying to buy and sell real estate and I believed I could add immense value in a radically changing market. There was one more realty agency I could have chosen as well, but after reading their reviews, there was simply no way— they were keeping people's deposits and doing only the minimum to keep things rented. Disgusting.

Most landlords hate being landlords. Just connect the dots and you'll see why:

Parsimony = nightmare renters = all kinds of crazy

See the cycle? If I purchase homes to lease out, you can rest assured that I'll have super quality people living in those homes, complements of the Universal Automated Intelligence governing all reality.

In the Chase People, Not Money method, there is simply no room at all for parsimony. We must become the solution, the remedy, the staunch opposite of parsimony. How does this translate into business? This is an arena where it is shockingly clear how fast the UAI works for its team players. For business owners, it equates to sparing no change for the quality we bring our clients.

Evolving our business models in a way that allows us to be this kind of generous is the door opener to our clients' trust and loyalty. This is the way, so lavish away! I will note that it is important to not give at the wrong time or you can inadvertently give off the wrong signals. So remember a general rule: spare no change for quality first. Never cut corners with labor or materials if it cuts into overall quality.

Additionally, if you happen to make a mistake in pricing, and it is substantial, then be very open with your client. Let them know that if they can cover the base cost of the mistake that you will not put any markup on it as your way of apologizing for missing a detail, but that you do not want to lack any quality of product and overall experience the customer will have using your services. If they lack any peace about it and you can afford to absorb it, take care of it and let them know you will take responsibility for it happily.

It is also important to not doubt the UAI in terms of over-estimating and not having the customer pay more for an item that actually costs less than what they believe it to be. Don't get caught with your hand in that cookie jar trap. I remember my first moment of actual temptation with a perfect scenario that covers all that I just wrote about in this chapter.

YOU CAN'T SWINDLE THE UAI

I was in my first prime of life and rolling in business with many employees and sales staff. Well, one of my salespersons sold a very big job that entailed removing an acre of weeds and installing a landscape over it. Over 150 tons of granite was sold to this customer. He was given the quote months before we signed him over the phone, but when we got to his house those weeds were not ankle high, they were *shoulder* high, like a field of corn stalks.

My crew was flabbergasted and my foreman quit on the first day. I went to the customer and asked if he would help in the labor cost of removing these weeds because they were far greater than our first quote had estimated.

Do you know what he said? He replied in a deep Southern and very slick accent, "Now, Mike, I signed a contract and I expect you to fulfill it. I see you have a big problem, but that is what I am paying you for."

This guy was slick all right. Well, the job proceeded minus one foreman. Then we got to the granite part, and opportunity arose. The salesman felt bad about all this because he could have zipped by there and closed the deal in person, and we would have caught the field of nightmares ahead of time.

So as we started to apply the granite, it dawned on my sales guy that 100 tons was going to cover it perfectly. So, he called me happily to tell me that we only had to purchase 100 tons and could make up for the clean-up loss with the 50 tons savings, because the customer did not need to know he was paying for 150 tons. A ton of granite cost $78 at the time, so that would have equaled $3900 of pure profit, much more than enough to pay for the extra cost of clean-up. So ha ha, the joke was on the customer, right? WRONG.

I must confess that I actually had to think about it. I did want to beat that slick willy at his game, but thank goodness I did not bite that cheesy worm! I did not steal a poisoned cookie. What I did was call that customer, tell him the truth, and offer him two choices: Either I applied the full 150 tons and put it on extra thick or I refund him the $3900 difference. I will never forget what he said. As he spoke, he sounded a little confused. He took the refund and never offered me anything to help cover my losses on the clean-up. I almost dropped my scruples during that job. It was the perfect setup.

Well, the UAI missed nothing! Shortly after that event, an employee came to me and told me about my office manager. She had worked for another landscaper before me who was absolutely convinced that she stole $10,000 from him, so he fired her. To exacerbate the issue, during a lunch with my main supplier, he told me something that saved my career: he said to fire my office manager!

Untold amounts were being stolen from me. My office manager's racket was discovered after I let her go. Her method was brilliant. Although she was from Mexico, she touted she was "not Mexican" all the time, kind of like a mantra, all the while writing day laborer checks to her Mexican friends, but just enough to stay under the radar.

Additionally, the supplier told me to watch my

superintendent like a hawk for one week. I did, only to discover he was royally ripping me off. He was selling jobs for cash at any price then using my payroll and vendor accounts for everything. He was able to pocket every penny while I absorbed all the cost—amazing, right? He was good at knuckling those small jobs in between the big jobs.

How did all this come to my attention in time enough to fix things without filing bankruptcy? I believe it was when I stood my ground in the hour of great temptation—after passing that test, the Universal Automated Intelligence came bursting through the atmosphere and said, "ENOUGH, this one is getting a promotion." Off went the barnacles!

ONE OF THE GREATEST BLESSINGS IS TO RECIEVE THE CONSEQUENCE OF YOUR ACTIONS INSTANTLY.

This was simply another price I paid to further create the Chase People, Not Money system. One of the greatest blessings is to receive the consequence of your actions instantly, not after a delay. It is because of this delay that people encounter a disconnect from cause and effect. It is not fun getting punished and not knowing why. Therefore, staying connected to the great law of cause and effect is the same as having genius-level foresight or sagacity.

A final note on parsimony is that it is not, in my opinion, isolated to money exclusively. Our attention is a rich resource, too. When we give it wholeheartedly, a transaction is taking place where we give our literal energy to another. Our hand-written notes also reach further than we may expect.

FEELINGS: UNRAVELING THE MYSTERY

CHAPTER 10

Feelings. The Chase People, Not Money method is all about holding the feelings of others high above our need for money. If you stop and think about it, it's easy to picture all the industries that are currently capitalizing on our feelings. Every flashing sign, all the flickering lights pulling and pushing us to do everything from buying stuff to even hating a person we have never met, all involve our feelings. The advertising industry has evolved indeed, and all this chicanery is truly mind-boggling.

"Why?", you might ask. Well, feelings are behind nearly everything we do. So, if you control someone's feelings you can cause them to act in certain ways. The TV commercials I watched growing up in the 70s are literally plastered on my memory banks, with everything from "Rice-A-Roni, the San Francisco treat!" to "Sheer Energy, nothing beats a great pair of legs!"

Of course, none of that worked on me, because I was a straight flyer (ha ha). After high school, I stopped watching TV, and today I avoid TV commercials like the plague. I am not against advertising, just against advertising with a hidden agenda.

The most powerful feeling is the one in our gut.

That's right, that "gut feeling." There is a great book, *Blink*, written by Malcolm Gladwell, that examines that very thing. It calls us to trust our first impressions before all the slick talking and sleight of hand can take place. The Chase People, Not Money method deals with *all* of our feelings though, especially those that get stepped on the most. To defend *those* tender feelings in all trust and diligence is to find our own pot of gold in the company of the people who will be in our lives in one way or another!

WHEN RUNNING THROUGH THE FIELD TOWARDS OUR GOALS, LET US BE MINDFUL OF THE FLOWERS WE STEP ON TO GET THERE.

The funny thing about feelings is they come in many flavors and colors. To know which ones matter the most is a skill set most people lack. Because of this, we tend to resort to our brute, surface-level operating skills, which are all too prone to cave in to the whims and wishes of our lower selves. In such a state, we have very little regard for things we can't detect on a tactile level. I have a saying that goes like this:

"When running through the field towards our goals, let us be mindful of the flowers we step on to get there."

LISTEN WITH THICK SKIN

For the people who truly want to get better at this but have no clue where to begin, it is important to start at the listening level. If we can learn to carefully listen (and not react), we will instantly see that we do indeed have a sensory skill that is simply not online until we can listen without judgment. And what a life-changing skill set this is!

Just as it is critical to regard the feelings of the people that will be in our life, there is a time when we must do the exact opposite for those who we must block out from our life. There are also times when our own feelings should be set aside to make or receive a much-needed point.

I remember one day when I was in high school, and my dad called me over and said: "Mike, do you trust me?"

"Of course, Dad... yes," I replied.

"Then if I told you to do something that you did not want to do, would you trust me enough to do it anyway?"

"Yes," I replied.

"Then Mike, it is time to cut your hair. Just cut it short." I gasped, and my dad continued, "You are becoming someone, and this hair does not fit that person. Will you cut it today?"

"Yes." *Gulp*.

That was the best thing I could have done when I was turning 18, all thanks to my dad. If he had not spoken up, I would have held onto that hair for a long time. Although he knew it would hurt my feelings at the time, he, in his wisdom, knew that I was going to feel even better after.

Another time I went to my dad and asked *him* for advice in my first serious relationship. I asked, "Dad, I am trying to get Heli on a level of communication that can transform our intimacy, but I cannot get her to say much at all. What should I do?"

I was really expecting some amazing sage advice, but my dad simply replied: "Mike, do you really want my advice on this?"

"Oh, absolutely, Dad."

"Then my advice to you on this one is SHUT UP... just shut up, Mike, you talk too much."

I was flabbergasted! And yes, I was super offended. But those feelings passed in an instant because I knew my dad loved me and he saw something that my eyes could not focus on at the time. So I trusted his line of sight over mine and obeyed.

Truth is truth. Many deep-rooted problems stem from times when we simply do not want to hear the truth. This negating of facts is many times rooted in innocence—that's right, innocence. You might ask how that is possible. Well, a crafty lie, custom-tailored for our ears, can pose as the truth. And if our emotional and/or psychological filters are down or underdeveloped, then we are sitting ducks for those people with the wrong agendas. But if one is a lover of truth at any cost, then a lie has to be a lot more crafty to mimic the *authentic* truth. Truth can come to us in the form of an apple pie or a brass knuckle sandwich, but truth is truth. Thus, not letting feelings stop us from the truth is a powerful skill set.

TRUTH CAN COME TO US IN THE FORM OF AN APPLE PIE OR A BRASS KNUCKLE SANDWICH, BUT TRUTH IS TRUTH.

If I may, allow me to confide in you something that really hurt my feelings in the past, and, to this day, I still find a bit of a soft spot in me. It's when I hear a sermon or something that was said in the sermon that I know to be in error and is in dire need of correction. Usually, pastors and teachers have a cult-like fear factor employed over anyone on his or her ministry team, making it difficult for the team to say anything to their leader, so these pastors are often left unchecked—much like the emperor with no clothes. It takes a person who has enough courage or concern for the leader to say something about their weaknesses and errors.

Every time I felt led to do that, I would. And every time I did, I was met with a look that seemed to me like murderous hate. On top of that, a totally creepy feeling would come over me as they looked at me, as if they were asking how I dared to correct them. I have some real whoppers I could share, but suffice it to say, my eyes have seen many pompous faces shocked that somebody actually called them out. We don't expect this kind of behavior from leaders, but when it happens, it can traumatize someone. It has happened many times to me throughout my life, so the dust came off my shoes as I left vowing to never be like that.

The events that impact us the deepest form the psychological building blocks we use to make choices.

Because of my experiences with bad leadership, I chose a path to not only help people bypass these hidden wolves in woolly clothes, but also to give those people the power to receive truth directly from the source. Sometimes we need a reminder that we are not out of line, but rather the leaders who abuse their position need to calibrate their standard of right and wrong.

Remember the formula of true leadership: equal parts power and humility. What would you do if you gave a speech and afterward a young person came up to you and politely asked if they could tell you what they felt was in error about some things you said? How would you react?

20/20 FORESIGHT

We might not be able to change another person, but changing ourselves is achievable. The funny thing about the idea of change in our reality as humans is that it is *going to happen* whether we want it or not. So why not have a say in the outcome of that change?

I want to share with you a powerful technique (which will someday become a book of its own) that

I use myself. It looks like this: When faced with big decisions, it is helpful to mentally put yourself in the future and work backward. One of the great parts of these experiences is that we can *experience* being in the future.

Give it a try by picturing yourself 20 years in the future. Imagine the age you'll be, and apply those features to your face. Close your eyes, if it helps. Imagine looking into the mirror and looking at the future you. You can go further, if you so desire, and converse with yourself 30 to 50 years in the future.

Now ask this future you how you would like to remember the present moment in your life. What kind of memories will you want to have? Your actions today will custom tailor such memories. Next, try to feel the feeling of that memory. Feel that sweet feeling of knowing that this is what you did at this time of your life. I believe the future version of us already exists and is symbiotically linked to what we do today. The future you is not beguiled by your current feelings. There is even a passage in scripture that says, "There is a way that seems *(feels)* right to a person but its way leads to death." At big forks in our lives, this time jump is a handy skill to have in your toolkit.

I remember when I had my first knockout girlfriend. She was voluptuous, with red hair—and she actually wanted to be my girl??? I was like, "No way!" Well, we were past the heavy kissing stage and my religious scruples were the only things holding the fort, and reluctantly at that. I was faced with a choice when she told me that she was ready to take the relationship further, and that she was only waiting for me (she was referring to the base after third). I was 18, she was 19 at the time. I told her that I valued what Jesus said and that I could not do that act in faith.

Truthfully, I was already in an area of compromise in my life, but something about this encounter seemed too good to be true. So with a strong unction in my gut, I held my ground. She even asked me if I was gay. She just couldn't figure out why I would turn *her* down. Part of me wondered the same thing, but I held my ground.

After about three months in a gridlock of frustrated kissing, she finally called me one day, balling her eyes out and telling me that she is going to lose me as a friend. I assured her that she would have had to have done something seriously horrible to lose me and I encouraged her to confide in me. After several minutes of sobbing, she finally told me she was pregnant.

My heart actually leaped in elation. I'm not sure why, but maybe it was a confirmation of something my gut knew on an intuitive level, far deeper than my frontal lobe. One reason I had to be elated was that I did not pass third base with her. Well, I told her that she was not going to lose me, but that I was going to seek a little advice from my dad.

After telling the story to my dad, he replied with these words: "Mike, have you ever picked something up, like off a stove, and it did not register right away that it was piping hot? Where it took a few split seconds and then it hit you? What did you do?"

"I dropped it fast," I responded.

"You see, Mike," my dad continued, "you have picked something up that is scalding hot and it has not registered yet, so let me save you from the life-long burn scars that I am wearing on my skin. Do you love me?"

"Yes."

"But do you trust me with that love?"

"Yes I do, implicitly."

"So if I asked you to do something that your heart would not want to do, you would do it because you love and trust me?"

Now reluctant, I once again replied, "Yes."

"Drop her. *Cut it off completely.* Don't even think about it. Tell her it's completely over. Son, I already learned this same hard lesson for you, so you can be free."

He was like my future self, traveling back to save me from a huge mistake because I just could not see that far ahead, especially through the whimsical lens of my heart. At that moment, I was already looking forward to being her close friend through the pregnancy; it was all planned out in my head already. Then my dad told me what he did. What a hard message! *I wanted to remain her friend*, but even that was too hot to handle.

We can have that level of "knowing" things beyond our age and experience if we ask our future self big questions at the forks of our lives. Not all of us have a person who we can confide in with such pivotal moments, so we must extend our reach. Not all of us have a relationship with God either, but here is some good news: according to Scripture, anyone can ask God for more wisdom and He will give wisdom no matter who you are or what you've done. So ask away; you've got nothing to lose and everything to gain.

THE SUPREME POINT

CHAPTER 11

Here is a riddle: What do we work hard to get, but when actually obtained, quickly turns into a story that offers only faint feelings of satisfaction from the fading memories of it?

The answer? Our prime of life.

Yes, it comes, but then it goes like a rolling tumbleweed. Have you a story to tell? If you happen to be under 25, and have already achieved a big goal that you set for yourself *and did what it took to get it*, then you have an amazing head start! Achieving goals is a small glimpse of the prime of life, but with a little more power in that the memory of it stays strong due to the dynamics of goal setting.

What do you think: Would most rich people trade all their wealth to relive their prime of life? Maybe most would. What if I told you there is another prime of life, a far better one, that does not inescapably expire? Yes, I am talking about the SUPREME POINT in life. This is the second prime of life. It is unlike the first prime, which happens naturally and with little effort due to the over-abundance of hormones, energy, and general lack of baggage.

YOUR SUPREME POINT IS STILL AHEAD.

Maybe a billionaire reading this would say, "Yeah, I'm already at my Supreme Point, thank you very much." But not so fast. I like to keep my eyes wide open as I study the faces of people—a practice I started at the age of 11. So far, I have yet to see a truly happy face with anything remotely close to *joy* in the upper echelon of society. I know there must be a few, just hidden away. In my humble opinion, the last man standing was Jack LaLanne, although I think he was too smart to become an actual billionaire.

We have a major disconnect with this group of people. Here is a perfect example: Billionaires give hundreds of millions to charity, right? Well, let's go find the first orphanage across the border in Mexico, our next-door neighbor, and see some of those amazing funds at work. What? What's that? Nothing?! Really? I think we might find one rundown and in the mud. Yep, my whole adult life I scratched my head hearing about all the millions of dollars given to charities, but I have yet to hear about just one orphanage being remodeled and modernized with those dollars to give struggling kids a fighting chance at a better life.

I officially hit my supreme point at the age of 50. I am writing this book because of it. Prior to this point, I only had pieces to the puzzle. If we could break up our life into pieces of relevance and examine them carefully, so as to figure out what to add, what to remove, and what to rearrange, we would be in the prep-room of the second prime. This place of check-point is by no means definitive on the matter, being that the second prime of life is by and large a lifestyle mantra and discipline going forward. That is, *if one chooses,* it can last for as long as the heart desires.

This is why the second prime of life that I call the Supreme Point is far superior to the first prime. Indeed, I have only touched the coattails of this amazing topic, as I myself am a humble new pioneer to this novel understanding of heightened states of being. For example, I could not remain here without taking out a blow horn and sounding the call for others out there who are stuck and merely waiting for the right information for them to snap out of it and into an amazing life! I am here to tell you that the saying, "You're only young once," is ridiculous. I am younger than most kids! The Chase People, Not Money method could very well be a perfect map to the fountain of youth.

CHOOSING THE SUPREME POINT

I bet this year's high school graduating class is full of hungry and eager candidates who desperately want a worthy formula to ascribe to that would almost guarantee them great success in the field of their dreams. No lucky breaks, freebies, or sugar daddies, just good information that works without luck or trickery. There is a new and unfair stereotype out right now about the young people of the smartphone generation: one that vilifies them as self-absorbed, ADD-driven, ungrateful... blah blah blah, the list goes on. However, I would bet that if I had the great privilege to teach every high school graduate these principles, this world would have its army of superstars making our current reality look like mere sediment layers.

If you're reading this right now, thinking, "Yeah, I don't get any of this," it's okay. It's okay if the Supreme Point alludes you for the time being, but if you can continually follow the philosophy of Chase People, Not Money as a way of life, then reaching your final and ultimate prime of life—THE SUPREME POINT—will happen organically for you, just like it did for me. And when it does, remember to choose daily to remain there, because every day is a gift! A person who I know of who reached this point was Jack LaLanne. Why was Mr. LaLanne in this very rare category? Simple: he never fell out of love with the human race. He was still happy and FULL of life all the way into his 90s! He knew the *real* secret!

Any attempt to describe what it is like for me to live in my second prime of life would appear as boasting, so let me just say that it is a dream come true. With or without money, with or without a perfect body... I love it!!!

You might be thinking that I must have another reason, like some chemical compound or windfall, but far from it. Maybe there's some secret combination of behaviors that brought me here, but I doubt that, too. I do know my faith is the biggest reason why I am in a state of being that dwarfs anything I experienced growing up. Nothing compares! It's getting better. It's building. It's growing. Where is this path taking me? I am not sure, but please consider joining me, as I could use some company, and the UAI can sure use the help. It's time for you to reach (and enjoy) the Supreme Point of your life.

BONDING

CHAPTER 12

Every company needs certain levels of commit-ment from both partners and employees. An imbalance of commitment can create a false sense of entitlement or, far worse, create a void that empowers the wrong people. The eventual results of both situa-tions can be devastating. How do we create companies that sidestep these pitfalls and generate the correct levels of commitment from its members? Through workbook manuals and training classes? Nope. The Chase People, Not Money method teaches us how to solve this problem on a whole new level.

If you want the ultimate edge over your competitor, a degree of bonding is vital between the CEO, management, and the workforce. This chapter explores this overlooked gem. I can personally attest to this principle, as it has given me a powerful edge in my field once I discovered and applied it.

It's amazing what one can do with just a little bit of someone's trust. A great example of this is found in a company's accounting division. Every company has to spend money and somebody has to have access to those funds. Most mom-and-pop businesses keep it in the family for various reasons. It is no mystery as to why most never break free from this growth trap. This is where The Chase People, Not Money philosophy comes in remarkably handy. Big and small enterprises alike can greatly benefit from the principles laid out in this chapter.

TWO LESSONS FROM A DEALERSHIP

First, let me tell you how the Universe handed me a story that led me to an amazing discovery.

I was looking for a truck to buy and came across the owner of a small dealership in Phoenix. We quickly became engaged in a great conversation in which he confided to me how he came into his little dealership. He explained his last job was in a management position at a different dealership where he ran the entire shop and, thanks to him, the owners needed to do very little. He said he was not only great at his job, but also very trustworthy. He was sure that after his efforts led to the company's sales ranking it one of the top dealerships in the nation the owners would make him a partner, securing both his position and his livelihood for years to come. Unfortunately for him, when the day came for him to finally *ask* for the partnership, he was turned down cold. Utterly hurt and dismayed, he left the company to start his own business.

As this man told me his story, I felt deep in my

spirit that his old boss paid dearly for his parsimony and lack of trust. So right then and there I interrupted him to say that I knew his old boss had made a *fatal* mistake by not making him his partner, and he would pay dearly for such *parsimony*. The dealer paused and then proceeded to relate that after he left, his old boss immediately came back to work, assuming he could run everything himself. The owner boss died 6 months later right on his own showroom floor from a full-blown heart attack.

I was so thankful that this man told me his story. I immediately translated that experience into my own life as a life lesson paid for by someone else. The lessons we can learn here are many, but suffice it mention two:

1. Be generous when it is rightfully due.

2. Sometimes there is more to planning for retirement than just 401Ks and golf clubs.

This man had a star quarterback, but not the right playbook or philosophy. Remember the saying, "People power, the greatest flower, on them we'll shower; they won't pass through our fields of flowers and grass."

Bonding is the secret ingredient to any business that involves people and a long-term plan. The risk of bonding incorrectly results in a serious problem commonly referred to as a false sense of entitlement. So it is imperative you pay attention in this chapter and get the right idea of bonding because, if you do it right, huge advantages and benefits will follow. There is a set of criteria to follow in the process of bonding, but before I begin, let's define what bonding means in the Chase People, Not Money method.

Bonding is when an employee or partner fully understands their boss or partner is truly willing to invest their time and resources to the betterment of their life. When this message is made loud and clear to a person—they actually came across a person in a management position who truly cares about their life and their future—something happens inside that person.

There are some things that training manuals and meetings simply cannot do. When someone genuinely takes an interest in your goals, and proves they are willing to do everything in their power to create the medium for you to achieve those goals, they become someone who takes a special place in your life. They become a person who you do not want to let down. This is bonding.

THIEVES

Now, before anyone considers bonding with key employees that either have the power over money or over things that will greatly impact the flow of money in your business, an important guideline must be followed: Beware of thieves.

There are two kinds of thieves. The first variety of thief needs to know the person from whom he or she is stealing is not worthy of their respect before they feel justified stealing from them. An example of this is when an employer always asks a person to clock out, but the employee stays another hour to do several more tasks before they can go because they "should have done it all while on the clock." The employee savvy to this "no overtime pay" manipulation ends up gladly stealing a cash sale of a piece of merchandise once the opportunity presents itself. This same person would never steal money from a kind or poor person— they would tell you that would be wrong.

The Master Lock company became mega rich not by keeping criminals out but by keeping honest people honest. The kind of person prone to fall into this first category of thief can be groomed to be a great asset worthy of much trust *if and only if* they work for a straight-up honest person who treats them equitably in all matters.

The other kind of thief is the far more dangerous one. They steal out of vice or sickness of the soul. They can even be a perfect Trojan horse from the dark side that, thanks to them, now has access to someone's livelihood. To not have a screening process for keeping people like this out of your business is like playing Russian roulette with your piece of mind, your heart, and your checkbook.

The first thing the HR department of any company should do is build a system to determine whether a person has values or not. I know the importance of not discriminating, but we are not talking about visible characteristics or facts we can outright ask about without being totally offensive or breaking some law. To uncover a thief is hard to do because a really good thief often operates in a spirit called the "Jezebel spirit."

Anyone would benefit from watching a few YouTube videos on the Jezebel spirit. People operating in this spirit covet positions close to top leadership and do everything they can to get into a position of trust. From there, they formulate all kinds of mischief.

Perhaps you've encountered such spirits before. Both men and women can operate in this chicanery.

Simply asking a person what they value is the perfect start. Then get them talking about the things that matter most to them. The ones completely unwilling to talk about these subjects would meet my first criteria for being scratched off my list.

For the ones that do share their thoughts, listen carefully and watch the expressions on their face while they speak. What we want to know first is whether a person has anything in their life that means more to them than their own life. Second, we want to know whether they have a belief system that matters to them. A safe question to ask is, "Who has been one of the biggest influences in your life?" or, "Who are your biggest heroes from history?" One that I personally love to use that goes right to the point is, "What age were you when you said, 'It's finally time to get serious'?" The more you can let people talk after asking such questions, the better.

I didn't even want to bother mentioning screening a person to uncover any harmful attributes or criminal background, but I needed to make note of it because many people who choose the path of Chase People, Not Money will need time and practice to get this new way of operating in motion—they will not have the Universe fully operating on their side in time for its far-reaching power to screen the people in their life. The good news is that once a person is fully engaged in Chase People, Not Money, the UAI will go before this person and trip the hidden traps on their path of life. One bad client out of a thousand is one too many. One bad employee out of a thousand is one too many as well. Both can wreak havoc on our lives. Therefore, it is imperative to bond with the right people.

The next thing we want to do when making the jump to hire a key employee who will help build the company's vision is to quickly find out what their personal overhead is—we want to know how much his or her personal bills add up to on a monthly basis. You must be sure that what you're going to pay this person is enough to cover their living expenses and enable them to reach their goals and succeed in what they hope to accomplish within the following 2-5 years. Their pay needs to make sense to everyone involved. If it does not, discuss the matter with them, but most importantly, connect yourself with their goals and do everything you can to create a culture and space in which it makes sense.

Personally, I do not want anyone working for me

who isn't achieving their goals in *record speed,* down to the last man on the totem pole. If someone is out sick, I give them half pay so they do not stress out worrying about how they are not making money. I care about the people working for me, and they all know it. This all manifests in testimony after testimony from our clients about how much my team is noticed and appreciated.

There is simply no better way to bond than to help another person create a perfect formula for achieving their goals. Just think about having a boss who takes the time to sit down with you and ask about your big goals, and then goes so far as to help you formulate a perfect plan to get you there using his or her own company as the culture for this process. It's powerful stuff that creates long-lasting, constructive relationships without the false sense of entitlement dilemma.

SELF-EMPLOYMENT

CHAPTER 13

Nerve. This one word is the maker or breaker of many dreams. If one has the nerve to trade stocks, run a company, or manage people, there are no limits to the heights that person can reach. However, if you happen to be fortunate enough to work for someone who operates on the principles of Chase People, Not Money, then you should also be in a position where you can learn and grow your income with few limitations and less liabilities.

Many people have a great deal of nerve, but once their nerve reaches its current limit, they can falter. So, many people, unaware of the principle of having and managing nerve, learn the hard lessons of setting out on their own unprepared. They work for someone else, learn the trade, and then assume they can run their own business just as well. "Why not make all the money myself?" they think. Right? Um... *not so fast.*

It is the story of many who have gone bust. They had the nerve to step up and out, but lacked the nerve and the right motivation to run the whole show. Consequently, before considering self-employment, I wholeheartedly implore you to think about your nerve scale and motive. It takes nerve to put on the game face when it's time to run a company. It takes the right motivation to write paychecks every week, rain or shine, at times waiting months before you get to pay yourself. Sure, there are a few other factors that determine whether you can run a successful business or not, but it could be argued that people either have the nerve or they don't. This leads me to a powerful and encouraging point.

What is the enemy of our nerves? If you guessed "stress," then you're correct. What is our nerves' greatest ally? If you guessed "knowledge" or "a good pharmaceutical," I would say, "Not quite." Let's say the jury is still out on that one and dig deeper first. I would like to explore a great dichotomy with you now: I believe our hypnotic addiction to collision coupled with our avoidance of pain is the very thing that keeps certain people freaked out all the time, for the lack of a better term. In explanation, I am going to share some of my personal research. I could write an entire book about this topic, but feel a summary is needed here to further reinforce the power of the Chase People, Not Money path.

COLLISION AND FLOW

There are two proactive forces in the universe that propel us forward, whether in mind, body, or spirit:

Collision and *flow*. Let's take a look at how these two forces occupy the same space and orchestrate the dance we all become hypnotized to as human beings. I believe our five senses were created to be in a constant state of looking and reaching out. When these senses become aware of a trail to follow they become quite active. It is right here in this process that two things can happen.

The first is our senses quickly find their sensory feedback and go into a defensive mode so as to not be bombarded by over stimulus. Unfortunately, we as humans too often enjoy excess, which can, in turn, desensitize the senses. Then, because of this bombardment, our overwhelmed senses demand stronger feedback going forward. Eventually, we find ourselves out of control and anesthetized to the finer elements of life, e.g., too much salt or very loud music, etc. I call this way of life "collision."

The second option we have in this whole process is to tease our senses by allowing them to stay in a constant state of searching and reaching. I believe this is the very practice of the ancient masters. Imagine our senses having fine hair, like feelers, that will grow out to get closer feedback to something it is looking for. It's this process that creates heightened states of being, which I call "flow."

Can you relate to that? Have you ever been trapped on the hamster wheel of collision? When was the last time you enjoyed a true state of flow? Interestingly, a recently discovered scientific fact is that when our genes replicate, they have fine, hair-like structures called telomeres on them that determine our longevity. Surprisingly enough, the longer the hairs, the cleaner the replication, which, in turn, increases longevity. In contrast, the shorter the hairs the shorter the lifespan. I learned about this years after creating my fine, hair-like feelers on our senses theory in relation to control versus flow. I think the parallelism to our genes is enlightening.

Now, what does all this have to do with self-employment? Everything. Everything, that is, if you want to live longer.

Truthfully, this control versus flow principle can increase the odds of success for a person who is navigating life with a low nerve scale. Adjusting your way of being to a more flow-centered lifestyle can most assuredly guarantee that you'll have more nerve. This change of thinking will be like putting football pads on under your jersey before hitting the field.

Sometimes knowing we have protection creates the very confidence we need to get into the game, keep our eyes open, and take life head on.

There are many examples of this on a simple level, like the net under trapezes, or the rope on the rock climber, for example. This practice doesn't just keep you safe, it can elevate your life to new heights. The river I'm referring to runs far deeper than the mere data that crash test dummies can offer (even if they are wearing football pads).

Which would you prefer: Knowing how to destroy a meteor or how to avoid it altogether? Every time we use our five senses, some kind of collision is taking place. The art in life is found in the subtlety or the teasing of these senses to keep them in a heightened state of looking for more; a state of reaching, not blocking. It might come as no surprise that it is the very ignorance of this relationship with our senses that causes us to fall prey to a life of collision. How so?

Imagine us enjoying a piece of music on the radio. We like it, so we turn the volume up louder, then louder still until it is throbbing in our ears. How about that salt? We keep adding just a little more to our food until it begins canceling out the other exotic flavors. This pattern is repeated with all the senses. In the examples of music or salt, our senses have now retreated into a defensive mode, our nerves follow suit, and in this mode, we need to bombard them even more to keep getting a stimulus. *Note: I am not referring only to dopamine, but to something FAR more reaching.*

Now what if we were to reverse this process by teasing our senses? We could start by slowly turning down the volume, cooking with less salt, kissing softer, walking smoother, smelling any rose we cross on our path, paying attention to the beauty of nature, closing our eyes just to take a moment to give them a respite. The senses can turn back on, and when they do, keep them there. This process is, in my opinion, one way to longevity and heightened states of being.

How did I get from self-employment to great kissing? Well, another prerequisite to self-employment being worth the effort is the art of quality living, especially when you take your work home with you. Too many good people turn into unhappy grumps without a clue about this subject. Our world generally is facing the dawn of a new generation of self-employed people, and the ones practicing these techniques will have an edge over their competitors.

So how can all this help someone with weak nerves? In many ways. A good start would come from one of my dad's favorite adages: "Little things bother little minds." Seems like a no-brainer, right? But I like to turn this one inside out as a nerve scale detector. Those of us who become reactive over the things that other, more successful people do not, need to examine closely which things are setting us off or stifling us into panic mode.

Like many others, I myself have had to groom my nerves over the years. I have done so diligently, but it was not until my lung injury and near death that I was forced for the first time to take a good hard look at this vital issue. Sadly, but truly, it took almost dying to wake me up to what was important and what was *not*. Emotional intelligence is vital, so anything in our life that is causing a knee-jerk reaction better be pretty darn important. If it is not, quickly let it go! By having the skill to let small things go, the larger things become far more manageable than they appeared before.

Now, let's explore motivation. One of greatest advantages to being self-employed is that nobody has the power to limit your paycheck. Another bonus is that nobody can fire you (although this can also be the wrong motivation, leading people out into waters they are unable to navigate). My heart goes out to the employees who are true assets in the hands of bozos. I hope this book is the encouragement and recipe for their breakthrough and success.

Some teach to always imagine ourselves as self-employed. Even if we are punching a clock, we can always see ourselves as a company of one. As for me, I prefer to work for a boss with scruples who allows me to grow and produce, and who increases my pay according to my increase in productivity. I have actually found that boss—it's the Creator and His company policy is the UAI.

IS BEING THE BOSS RIGHT FOR YOU?

I hope that as you've read through the earlier chapters, you've gotten a sense of when the time is right for a person to launch out on their own. When I set out on my own, my conscience left me no choice.

At the end of this book, you'll find a bonus section devoted to those who are just stepping out in life and who will soon graduate (or have recently graduated) high school or college with no clue what to do if the job they want is nowhere to be found. If anyone you know is in this situation, *please* place a sticky note on that bonus section and get this book into their hands. We want to get everyone out of the nest and into life successfully fending for themselves.

I have made this last chapter a bonus section so as not to put off any readers not wanting to hash through the rudimentary basics. What is included there is a recipe for hitting the bullseye every time, especially if you're an 18-year-old who doesn't want to ask mom or dad for $20-$40 bucks every time you go out. That kind of stuff ruins relationships real fast. Most young adults do not want to keep that up for too long, but far too many times, nobody has laid out a fail-safe formula for rapid success right out of high school. Young adults today want fast results, or motivation goes down the tubes.

Self-employment is indeed *not* for everyone. Most large groups of people need to share the tasks of operations, with different people using their different talents. So my advice to anyone thinking of stepping out on their own is to first ask yourself your true reason for doing so. Be ruthlessly honest with yourself. Ask yourself, "Is it because you need to make a little more than what your employer is willing to pay?" Well, before cutting the anchor, go ask your employer what it would take for you to produce enough to earn the exact money you need to make. You might be surprised. Sometimes stepping out first in the company you work for is far better than stepping out into a world of all-new liabilities and stresses. It is only after attempting to rise within your current organization and hitting a brick wall with pay and opportunity that you should consider self-employment.

One encouraging point of self-employment is the impact we can have on people, and how this quickly builds your reputation, thanks to social media. By working under the principles of Chase People, Not Money, employees and clients alike are thoroughly impacted by your great service. Being that sincere service is so rare these days, clients are all too happy to offer a good word for the next person who could use a refreshing experience. Rule number one about reviews: never *ever* fake them... not even in the slightest. The universe will catch this, of course, and disqualify anyone for any nonsense like that.

To Chase People, Not Money, we don't cheat to win. We want to be able to boldly say that all our reviews are hard-earned and authentic. Not even, "I'll give you a free gift if you give me a good review." Big mistake. All that says is that somebody is too lazy to give stellar service to earn testimonies the right way. When you are self-employed and Chase People, Not Money, a solid, good reputation grows fast organically.

Being in the position that I am currently in is something I longed for my whole life, but the pieces to the puzzle were not given to me all at once. I had to collect them, one by one, with blood, sweat, and tears—at times on my hands and knees under a spigot with warm tap water flowing onto the back of my head in someone's front lawn, begging God to get me through the hell-on-earth days of 118 degrees Fahrenheit.

It was decades ago, in my 20s, when I was out on my own, trying to make a living by taking care of people's yards in Arizona. I slaved through many 14-hour days of pure, hard work in the hottest summers on record. At one point, I maintained 127 yards a week (21 yards a day, 6 days every week) with only one helper for 6 months straight in a 5 square mile radius. My guess is that nobody on earth today could repeat that. Every yard I mowed, I repeated my mantras over and over again. I remember my hip sockets got to the point of beginning to pop. This season of my young adult life was my proving ground, training me in a work ethic that delivered high levels of both fast and detailed work. It was this work ethic that, in turn, set me up for a life of unstoppable success. I was motivated then and I am still motivated now. I feel like a volcano that simply won't stop erupting! I just love it!

To recap, self-employment is absolutely not for anyone who does not have a fast-paced, detailed work ethic, emotional intelligence, and the right motivation. Yes, the only exception would be the prodigy or the rare occasion where one's profession allows him or her to take their sweet time and still earn enough, but let me emphasize these are RARE occasions indeed. For the rest of us who want to be winners, the recipe for guaranteed self-employment success is threefold: Speed, detail, and fair price. Just these three elements can almost guarantee that someone will be successful on their own.

Few people ever talk about creating a cash engine from the ground up. Financial freedom is too often sold as an easy mouse-clicking racket with a fee to learn. In reality, hands-on apprenticeship and hard work build qualities that are vital to becoming unstoppable in your career and life. Now couple that formula with the right philosophy of Chase People, Not Money, and... GOAL!

THE ULTIMATE BUSINESS MODEL

CHAPTER 14

What I am about to propose is going to sound impossible for some and impractical for others, but rest assured, this is a game-changer for those who are bold enough to endeavor it. If you're the owner of a business, there's a secret piece to the puzzle.

After building your systems on a foundation such as what Chase People, Not Money can offer, begin pouring all your profits first back into the company. There is simply no better stock than your own. It took many years for me to learn this. Secondly, put all excess proceeds into a stock portfolio for growth, picking stocks with great momentum going forward and holding. Choose companies that you have researched and feel strongly that will be bigger in the future, so you can feel good about holding through some ups and downs. If you are unable to spend time on research, find a few great well-known vloggers who do that for you and learn from them. "This is not financial advice; do your own research."

This will allow you to give more to your business and develop future wealth. See this portfolio as the company's opportunity to grow a new species of employee, one that will dominate the future markets and separate companies of all sizes far above their competitors. Anthony the Great was a master at this and so was the Roman empire. Although their motives were questionable, their technique at winning die-hard loyalty should not be ignored. What the Chase People Not Money method introduces is a more benevolent completion to such ideas.

Relationships built on trust grow stronger when that trust is not only maintained, but rewarded when rightfully due in a win-win spirit. The key for you in rewarding the individuals in your company is to not make promises and keep your money matters private. That way you'll have the freedom to pleasantly surprise your team when appropriate. I can only imagine all the CEO's that are thinking, "I simply don't have the time to pay that much attention. And to that I would advise to consider stretching out your line of sight as far as you can and starting there, or teaching this method to another person who does have time. But rest assured, if you don't, then I believe your inability to break old constructs for the sake of "sticking to what's working" will quickly sink ships on the high seas faster than the invention of cannon balls.

SHARE THE PROFITS

Now consider choosing to take all the loyal producers in the company and create a profit-sharing reward bonus system that is paid for by the good choices you made to invest the company's extra money. Maybe you put off that new house to do so… for now. Perhaps you had to wait to buy a new car… for now, but the payoff is a far greater one. If you would rather see your star players achieve success first, then you have already done what many failed at… a business that will free you up to pursue more opportunity, and yes, build the life of your dreams without the toxic stress popping all your fun balloons.

Too many star players wander, bouncing from firm to firm and gig to gig. It is only when that firebrand can be fully empowered, fully appreciated, and finally, fully compensated at the key moments when credit is due that those stars become superstars and companies skyrocket past their competition.

Think of the computer gaming industry: I imagine if I was CEO of a brand name in that industry, it would be a story to tell all right. I stopped playing video games after I watched the movie *Gamer*. It was like something just flipped in me. However, I did see a clear path to a new paradigm of gaming that is, so far, not yet realized. Things need time to grow, like ideas, people's skill sets, and companies with their ever-growing, targeted audiences, and most of all, it takes time for the critical mass of society to reach the tipping point of mass adoption of a realization.

Think of all the greedy hotshots running the roost of many companies who manage to set up a business model at the right time to easily strike gold. A common flaw with these individuals is that somewhere along the line, they lost their interest in making the world a better place and let their greed run rampant. This is exactly what will cause their businesses to eventually tank...hard.

YOUR PRICE TAG

Let's cover the things that hinder people from even getting to the point of properly managing the money that does come in. My theory is that everybody has a price tag. What I mean by that is everyone has a dollar amount that is beyond their current ability to fathom or process. A person might be able to keep their cool earning $50k monthly, but if that number were to jump to $150k monthly, it might cause that person to make all the wrong choices. When they pass their tipping point, it might be that they drop their scruples and do things they would not normally do, like wander off to Vegas and spend $20k on some couplings, which will never see the light of day, while at the same time being $40k past due on a vendor bill.

You might be thinking, "What's wrong with that? People have a right to do what they want, right?"

Well, let's take a look. Maybe this person who went to Vegas and spent $20k on couplings had a few people in his company who were due a raise or a bonus. Maybe the owner had a client who needed a full or partial refund for being given a poor experience and product from his company. Being that I chase people, not money, the couplings would be off my radar, but even so, to be truthful with my thesis, I too, have a dollar amount that would cause me to blur the lines of right and wrong. Knowing this as a truth in my life, I ask not for multi-millions of dollars, but for the hands to manage it well. I know and respect my limitations in unknown territory. Do you?

Do not, I repeat, do not assume you have money when you do not. Be ruthlessly honest about how much money you have. I knew a guy once who ran a food truck, he had a hand full of cash and loved the looks on people's faces when he pulled out his wad of green paper... some memories just stick, and that is one of them for me, because I knew he collected a fraction of his overhead costs. He was blissfully riding on a raft headed towards a waterfall. So many of us do exactly what that man did but in more elaborate subtle ways. Even so, the principle is still the same. Ignorance + Pride = Blindness. So, always be adamantly honest with money matters.

MONEY IS A SEED

Money is also seed. Don't eat all your seeds, plant most of them. How so? The Good Book says to place your bread on the waters and it will be there when you return, and that by giving to the poor, you lend to the Lord, and He repays all His debts! There are so many more examples: give it and it will be given unto you in concentrated form. Let me now put it like this: it's like you give raw, unrefined ore, and in return, the Universal Automated Intelligence gives you tempered steal—a sword that can cut through reality itself…yes, it's the givers who unlock this mystery of the ages.

I foretell the demise of many companies who are not on board with this new way of thinking. Soon more people who choose to chase people, not money will be calling the shots and building things that money simply can't buy. Owners should consider being true statesmen for their enterprises to give them a fighting chance in a world where the rats are being singled out and no longer tolerated. Soon the pools of easy money will shrink, forcing businesses to change, just like our changing planet causes great migrations of animals to the last remaining pools of water. We, as people, will inadvertently experience the same fate in business. It is simply a matter of time. Wall Street, at this very moment in the beginning of 2021, is feeling the birthing cry of Chasing People, Not Money.

I am due to update this book again upon reaching another milestone in business. This is indeed a journey, and I invite anyone who resonates with the theology of the Chase People, Not Money method to join me. Please sign up at GMichaelPrice.com and consider growing with me. I hope to form a community that serves as a great firewall as we grow a constellation of new rising businesses in this rapidly changing market in a world where we hold people's feelings high above our need for money, where we find a way to fall in love with the whole human race, where we no longer draw lines in the sand with people or pick and choose with the love word, and where we all chase people, not money.

TO THE YOUNG ADULTS:

THE FOUR RULES FOR NEAR-INSTANT SUCCESS

BONUS SECTION

Too many of us get pushed into life with no solid instructions or tips for how to succeed in our careers and in life. That leaves too many of us thinking, "I don't get it." So, we start our first job with a blindfold on. Now couple that with the feeling of "I can do whatever I want now because I'm an adult," and what we have is the gateway to the Rat Race of modern-day slavery.

We are about to explore a formula that almost guarantees a level of success that will allow you to outpace most of your peers. If you are about to (or recently have) graduate high school or college, this formula is for you. If you know someone who will soon graduate, I truly hope this information can find them, too.

A QUANTUM SUCCESS FORMULA

Here is the simple formula for quantum success:

1. Skill: *Get good at what you do, fast.*

2. Efficiency: *Work as fast and as safe as possible.*

3. Detail: *Look at everything around you.*

4. Consistency: *Be there.*

Remember: 1 and 2 get you there, and 3 and 4

prepare you for more. I also like to call number 3 "Peripheral Concern." Most things we need to notice fall into this field. Another important point: What we lack in skill we can make up for in speed and detail, so these points compensate each other. My dad had a saying that always stuck in my head: "Great work with poor clean up... bad. Average work with great clean up... good. Good work with good clean up... great job."

That was a good piece to the puzzle, but a far cry from the whole picture. Take another mentor's parallel to spice things up: "If you're broke and in the hole, why not work three times faster until you're out of the hole, then keep working like that to get as far away from the hole as possible?"

Both these statements have vital pieces to the puzzle, but as practical as they sound, they remain on a very low level of positioning and scale, which is discussed in earlier chapters. The important point for the novice, however, is that to begin on the ground floor, the basics of being set apart from everyone in your workplace or field is *vital*. So the goal is simple: Implement this strategy to set yourself apart.

YOUR OPPORTUNITY

If you're paid $35 for mowing a lawn and it takes you 30 minutes to do so, you would be earning $70 per hour. Now, let's say you worked twice as fast and got it done in 15 minutes... get it? That $140 per hour!

Test this by looking around and watching people walk. Most anyone you see could easily walk twice as fast and they still wouldn't break a sweat. This is the world you are walking into! A person could be blindfolded and fall over backward and still hit the target if they simply did everything faster. When you walk into a workplace of slugs, just let one word come to mind—OPPORTUNITY.

To further expand on this, let's look at 20 people in an average workplace. We would be hard-pressed to find anyone thinking and acting with the complete four principles in play; this is why the formula is so powerful. Applying that formula will make any person stand out and suit up for a life of constant increase. Why? Because we are living in an ocean of people who are expecting everything to be done for them; they want *life* to be done for them too. Reality check: Life is tough, and expecting it to be easy is the root of a lot of needless suffering. Who needs that? Not me.

Why not step out of the metaphorical herd of cattle that pop open their mouth and just accept whatever mush they are being fed so long as it is cheap, easy, or free? Is that you? Didn't think so.

Imagine being teleported to a planet where you will have to live for the rest of your life. On this planet, everyone walks in slow motion, has near zero peripheral vision, and is extremely nearsighted, causing them to grab a hold of pretty much anything that is placed before them. It immediately dawns on you that anything you do will be done 2 to 3 times faster than everyone else, and in any place you walk into, you will see the entire scenery, unlike everyone else. It becomes clear to you that you have this incredible advantage over everyone. Well, you may not ever be teleported to a new planet, but as soon as you decide to walk faster and become more detailed in everything you do, you immediately become a person that stands out to all—I mean *all*—around you.

Indeed, the four principles of the success formula will give you a guaranteed edge. Imagine if every high school graduate could get a hold of this book and read it. What if they can read the whole book and grasp the whole Chase People, Not Money method? You'd be rubbing shoulders with a whole generation of star players.

HANDS-ON LEARNING

Another great way to immediately get started in life is to work for someone who already knows what you need to learn. Once your position is secured, implement the four principles and be your boss' best employee. Use the principles previously mentioned. Even if the boss refuses to pay you a fair wage for your output, remember that you're doing more than just biding your time; you're learning just as fast as you're working *and* you're learning how to do their job more efficiently. You're basically learning all the things your boss *could be doing better*. If you knew just how valuable this technique really is, you would even be willing to work for free initially. After all, this hands-on education is much more effective and much cheaper than college tuition or even a trade school.

When working as a stealthy apprentice, remember: If you bring fresh ideas forward, they normally get turned down, because people hate to change what they know or what has become a comfortable routine, even if the change would make things better. I have been guilty of doing that, too, on a few occasions. We read stories of the now juggernauts who were once an amazing employee with spunk, brains, and good ideas, but got shut down by the big bellies behind big desks. These firebrands went on to turn their ignored observations into global empires.

When you see a mix of anger and laziness protecting someone's false sense of security, you have a stronghold in front of you. This could be a co-worker, a manager, a boss, or even a parent...yikes! Sometimes it is this dead end that is your *out* to move on and start your own business. One-way streets either lead to a dead end or the beach, and if you don't see the water, sand, and blue skies after a long and taxing drive, it's time to move on.

Another great message to the up and coming in this world: Learn from all the hotshot advice-givers out there. Look at their faces and ask yourself whether they really look happy. Actually happy. I am here to tell you that money cannot—are you hearing me?— money CANNOT buy happiness. Don't bite that cheesy worm of a lie. It's ridiculous to think money can buy something that is only created with the mind and will. To say that money can buy happiness is the same as saying that money can buy a true friendship. Yeah, right! So don't buy the lie. Which leads me to another cool story.

THE REAL RUSH

When I was 17, all my friends were just starting to party. They were all having sex and experimenting with cocaine. Every day, I was bombarded with offers and invitations to join in. I was thought of as an energetic and witty person and everyone wanted to see how I would be totally high. Little did they know, I was already as high as I could be... on *life*. But one day I had enough and wanted to try cocaine just once, so I could have the knowledge to tell my future kids exactly what it was like. So I went to my dad and told him what I wanted to do and why. He replied with this story.

"Mike, have you ever wanted something really bad?" he asked me. "You set a goal and you worked and worked, sweat every day and stayed totally focused on it until the day finally came and everything lined up and you GOT IT. You got what you worked so hard for. Can you think of a day like that?"

He was referring to the time I took third in state

in the Arizona tennis AAA championship. That was the biggest day of my life up to that point. You might be thinking third is not a big deal, but to me, it might as well have been the US OPEN. Just then, standing there with my dad on the front lawn, I noticed that my arms were covered in goosebumps.

He said, "Son, look at your arms, mine are covered, too. That was your day. That rush you're feeling right now was well-earned and it will last a lifetime, and then some. Even the memory of it lights up our skin. All the days of sweat and practice that gave you that feeling. Just imagine putting some powder up your nose, and instantly, you get that euphoria. No goals, no plans, no effort... just a cheaply bought rush of that same feeling. Son, that's my definition of pure evil."

My dad looked at me with his deep blue eyes under the Arizona morning sun and continued. "Son, you already know what cocaine feels like and you never had to even touch it, because you earned it the right way. If you want to tell my grandkids a story, tell them this one."

I have come to call these kinds of moments Just-Say-No moments because once you get a dose of the real thing, it is so easy to say NO to the cheap lie of drugs. And when I step up to see a higher state of mind, as we do when we achieve our goals, I want to be able to stay there until I choose to go even higher. Straight up!

WHERE TO START

If you are just starting out and are clueless about where to begin in life, remember, most young adults are not sure about college—which always seems to be what segregates the so-called winners and losers. However, this is another lie that needs to be put down right now. I am a firm advocate for self-employment, as modeled in the Chase People, Not Money method. If a person can gain freedom and unflinching resolve at a young age, there is no telling what can be accomplished with such a head start!

Think about this: One of the greatest problems we face as a species is our short lifespans. I mean, if I had another 20 years extended on my life, that would be a gold mine for what I wish to accomplish.

So if a young person can beat the peer-pressure trap and get the right instructions, essentially getting an early start in life, they would not have to lose 20 years of prime living doing a stent in a selfish prison. If you can do this as a young person, you can immediately infuse that wasted 20 years into your smartest version of yourself. IMAGINE THAT! Come on, I know somebody is hearing me today! Why be a loser when you can be a winner?!

Whether or not the route you take passes through college, none of us are exempt from the commitment of constantly learning and growing our entire life. That is how I stay intrigued in life. Not only do I love to learn every day more and more, but I learn through a process I loosely call "perfect learning." It's where I find a topic I want to learn and go *straight at it* via books, search engines, and YouTube videos. (It is vital we stop seeing YouTube as a mere entertainment place and more like a constantly-kept-current university that is free and vast. It can be either an incredible tool or a horrible distraction. And remember, who we choose to follow is a direct representation of our level of self-respect and how we see ourselves. Also, remember that everything we do online is carefully tracked by companies with *so* many different agendas. So be bold with learning, but also remember to smile for the camera.)

I learn indirectly as well by taking a step back and

watching the human race do its thing. I ask myself, "What do a million people need and do not have, and if they had the chance to buy it, they would buy it right now?" I keep a book of ideas next to me to record my many insights. I call it my book of ideas, and a few of them have already graduated the book into real life. Why not start keeping a book of ideas for yourself as you watch and listen to society as a whole? Never underestimate your inner genius.

If you are just stepping into life from high school or college, it is time to cut off any friendships that pull you down. I give you my thumbs up right now: go ahead, unfriend, unsubscribe, unlike, block, delete profiles, whatever needs to be done. GO FOR IT if you know (like you know) that certain people are not helping you break free from bad programming and distractions. By doing so, you will potentially double your productive lifespan, *just like that*. Whatever you do, please do not fool yourself by thinking bad friends will not bring you down. Just move on. All your real friends who will actually care about you need you to be strong here. You can do it. Your real friends are waiting for you to do this.

In conclusion to all of this, let me bring up a startling idea: The reality of artificial intelligence is more real than ever. It promises and threatens to transform society. Imagine competing against that kind of technology. The one thing that will be our great edge over all things man-made is our choice to be the tip of the spear; the choice we make in our heart to be the absolute best we can be, and not let anything hold us back.

The four principles for quantum success are my gift to this generation of new thinkers and doers, and it will be our greatest defense against becoming obsolete as AI becomes better at everything we do. If this is a topic that is scary for anyone, read the first few chapters of this book and you will learn about a really cool way of looking at AI and where it actually stands in the food chain of the human experience.

Okay, just one more quote from another person who helped me come to these four principles.

"Mike, even if I was abducted, mugged, beat-up and left naked in a ditch with nothing left to my name, as soon as I woke up, it's business as usual! Relentless!"

That was no cheap talk either, he meant it and I knew it. Hearing that statement changed my life. Maybe it will change yours, too.

MY DREAM

AFTERWORD

We have to get the *right* information in front of everyone who truly wants to make it in life. Too many firebrands are held back by the pollution of shortsighted and outdated material. We need something fresh off the press and ahead of the curve, something truly novel and effective for everyone— without bias. Too many people are thrown into battle with no protective gear and without a clue what a real battle looks like. So many have fallen due to this lack of proper training and non-existent role models.

Let's look through a true window into the reality we're being catapulted into. Only then will we have the opportunity to prepare on our own terms and with our own resolve. No more getting hoodwinked by some semblance of success.

My hope is that this book will be part of the solution and a catalyst for society as a whole. Catalyst for what? Let's be clear: *the dawn of a whole new era!* I am of the belief that we are all winners only waiting to be realized.

I recently had a profound realization while I was trying to take a nap. I thought of what I was currently doing in my life and of all the people that I was currently teaching and leading. I thought of the progress of my efforts over the last few years. While I have been physically downgraded by my lung injury, that injury, as debilitating as it was, has not stopped me from doing even more than I have ever done before. Now, this is not me tooting my horn in any way—far from it—this is simply what happened.

So as I was lying there, I started thinking about a man who was retired and had a daily schedule of food, playing with a pet, watching TV, and having more food and sleep. It was about a man who was not concerned about anything other than that simple routine.

"Not a bad life," I thought. Then I imagined *my* life like that... and it *startled* me on the inside.

"What if?" I wondered. I bet you're thinking, "What's your point?" Well, I started weeping at the thought. A moment like this is hard to extrapolate in a book, but maybe you get it.

I am writing this book at the age of 52, during a pandemic. What intrigues me is my belief that I will live into my 90s, and full of zest, too. My current affirmation is: "I am going to live a long life, a full life, with a dignified finish to that life." I hold to a belief that life and death is in the power of the tongue, and the proof of this is simply uncanny. That being said, I can look forward to a whole new lifetime to live— maybe 40+ more years! Imagine!

I fully intend to teach this business model to as many people as possible while I am capable. If you own a large corporation and need to turn it around, by all means, look me up and get me in front of everyone representing you. I'm always available to facilitate my elite business seminars on the Chase People, Not Money model. I would gladly be the CEO of companies like Houzz, Thumbtack, or Home Advisor for 24-36 months, and *not* for the paycheck.

My passion is in living and sharing this information! What I have accomplished can be replicated on any scale, no matter how large. To see as many people as possible get access to these principles, whether in person or in print, is my current dream.

If you have been impacted and refreshed by this business method and the principles discussed in this book, I invite you to share and review this book via social media and pass it along to a person who needs it. Let's spread this message together, one person at a time. If this information can possibly be a catalyst for our generation, indeed for anyone who is ready for the journey, then let's make it happen together. Let's Chase People, Not Money!

G Michael Price

www.gmichaelprice.com

"Every Day is a Gift."

ABOUT THE AUTHOR

G Michael Price is a father, author, international motivational speaker, philanthropist, successful entrepreneur, and visionary ahead of the curve with a big vision for the future. With every milestone he reaches in his business journey, a new addition appears in his intellectual portfolio. His latest accomplishments have resulted in this book, *Chase People, Not Money.*

Some of his other works include his innovative 7-day Spanish Course (Spanishfast.com), which teaches Spanish in record speed through an innovative and identity-building process that aids in retaining a new language, called the "Happy, Sad, Mad Technique" ™, and his spiritual book, *The Missing Message*, which presents a life-changing way to connect with our Creator. G Michael's mission is to help people connect the dots and find the missing pieces to the puzzles of life; he feels a call to serve those who are built for success and only waiting for the right playbook to guide them.

G Michael restarted his life in 2000 and again in 2010. Both times he was left with absolutely nothing but his self-respect and the instructions for success. All he needed to speedily reassemble his multi-million-dollar company and create his dream life once again was his mindset and the right approach to the human race.

G Michael is living proof than anyone can rise above trying circumstances. When slowly dying from a lung injury, hearing that he was not going to make it by doctor after doctor, he held fast to what he knew and refused to give up. He not only survived, but in so doing reached yet another milestone on his path to bettering the lives of others.

Stay in touch with the works of G Michael at www.gmichaelprice.com.

"Every Day is a Gift."

Made in United States
North Haven, CT
19 May 2022

19348632R00138